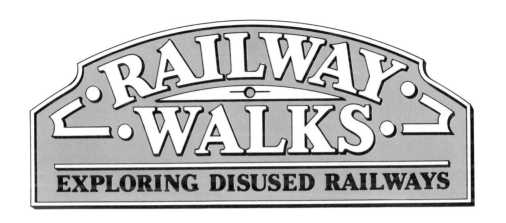

RAILWAY WALKS

EXPLORING DISUSED RAILWAYS

GARETH LOVETT JONES

DAVID & CHARLES
Newton Abbot   London   North Pomfret (Vt)

The author and publishers wish to emphasise that walkers should gain permission from the owner before entering any private land.

British Library Cataloguing in Publication Data
Jones, Gareth Lovett
  Railway Walks.—2nd ed.
  1. Railroads—Great Britain—Abandonment
  I. Title
  385' .0941   HE3014
ISBN 0-7153-8543-7

First published by Pierrot Publishing Ltd 1980
This amended edition published by David & Charles (Publishers) Limited 1983

Printed and bound in Great Britain by
The Pitman Press, Bath
for David & Charles (Publishers) Limited
Brunel House Newton Abbot Devon

Published in the United States of America by
David & Charles Inc
North Pomfret Vermont 05053 USA

CONTENTS

PART ONE: INTRODUCTION	9
PART TWO: NEW USES FOR OLD RAILWAYS	23
PART THREE: EXPLORATIONS:	53
The Bridport Railway	54
The Somerset and Dorset Joint Railway	66
The Midland and South Western Junction Railway	78
The Didcot, Newbury and Southampton Junction Railway	90
The Muswell Hill Railway	100
The Wells and Fakenham Railway	106
The Colchester, Stour Valley, Sudbury & Halstead Railway	114
The Rugby and Stamford Railway	122
The Kingswinford Branch	132
The Cleobury Mortimer and Ditton Priors Light Railway	138
The Severn Valley Railway	148
The Cromford and High Peak Railway	156
The Parkgate, Chester and Birkenhead Junction Railway	168
The Malton and Driffield Railway	178
The Eston Branch and the Castle Eden Branch	186
The South Durham and Lancashire Union Railway	196
The Border Counties Railway	206
The Bala and Festiniog Railway	214
The Dolgellau Branch	224
The Brecon and Merthyr Tydfil Junction Railway	232
The Last Resting Place?	244
PART FOUR: PUBLIC ACCESS TO DISUSED RAILWAYS	255
APPENDIX	278
FURTHER READING	282

'No more will I go from Blandford Forum and Mortehoe
On the slow train from Midsomer Norton and Mumby Road.
No churns, no porter, no cat on a seat
At Chorlton-cum-Hardy or Chester-le-Street.
We won't be meeting again
On the Slow Train. . . .

'The Sleepers sleep at Audlem and Ambergate.
No passenger waits on Chittering platform or Cheslyn Hay.
No one departs, no one arrives
From Selby to Goole, from St. Erth to St. Ives.
They've all passed out of our lives
On the Slow Train. . . .'

Michael Flanders and Donald Swann,
lyrics for 'The Slow Train.'

'WHERE THERE'S A RAIL, THERE'S A WAY.'

. . . Or so they believed in the 1840's and 1850's. The motto of this book might read 'Where the rails have been taken up, there still remains a way,' at least until such time as someone truncates the route forever by building a factory or a housing estate across the trackbed.

This is not a guide to the disused railways of England and Wales. Even if such a massive survey were viable, which seems unlikely, it would become immediately out of date: the fate of any one disused branch line is never absolutely fixed for the long term until the whole of its length has been reused for one purpose or another, and to date there are very few old lines which have evolved that far. Rather it is, as the title implies, an exploration of territory that is largely unknown to most people, even railwaymen, in its new post-closure form. Largely unknown to me, I must also mention, even before closure. I can certainly remember the steam trains, since my grandparents' house overlooked the station at Wellington in Shropshire, and I still have a particularly vivid recollection of my grandmother running into the garden to get her washing in when the wind blew the smoke over, as it generally seemed to do on washing days – a picture of silhouettes of grey-white sheets in clouds of smoke obliterating the sky, and a small figure grabbing them as quickly as she could whilst the house thundered with the engine noise. But despite that proximity railways never became a natural part of my life: I may have watched the trains over the garden fence but I did not become a train spotter, and more often I actually travelled by car, or bus, or bicycle, until such time as the steam locomotives had disappeared from public service forever. Then I began dimly to realise what it was that I had missed.

I have not attempted to provide a chain-by-chain account of the twenty lines and related sections investigated: partly because of the problem of dating; partly because as a photographer I was more concerned with doing justice to the appearance of the lines as they exist now and catching something of their individual quality as places (and disused railways are definitely *places*); and partly because I believe that the comprehensive predigestion of experience which has become the normal function of guide books can only take the freshness out of the actual discovery of whatever is being described.

I have set out, then, to produce a book which would stimulate an appetite for exploration in those who had not thought of disused railways as places to explore, and to sharpen it in those who had. Deliberately, I did not walk particularly lengthy stretches of line, and on several lines I did not even walk the stretch in a single piece, but moved around from location to location in order to make use of the best light whilst it was there. If you go to these places, you are very likely to discover things I did not see: therein I hope lies a part of the pleasure. You may also – be warned – find bridges out that I did not spot, or undergrowth that has knitted together since I was there.

The photographs themselves, like all photographs but noticeably so with such a subject, are ephemera, records of passing moments in places that will in many instances return to wilderness, and will in others disappear under cement and tarmac. What I hope the pictures do record, thirty-two years after the nationalisation of the railways, and seventeen years post-Beeching, is a transitional stage in the 'after-life' of the truncated lesser branches of a tree which had flourished as arguably the most comprehensive rail network in the world. As might be expected, the degrees of transition vary enormously from line to line. Some lines are still perfectly recognisable as one-time railways: the ballast remains down, holding back the weeds, the buildings stand, albeit in a ruinous state. But others are more than half grown over, or are in the process of being converted back into arable land, or have vanished entirely beneath new roads. The engineering of railways is so massive that it is highly unlikely that all will finally merge into a remade landscape; even more unlikely now that – at long last – the move in some counties towards converting railways into public paths is actually bearing fruit. Even so there were many times in my investigations when I felt more like an archaeologist than a casual explorer of tangible remains. Civilisations change faster than most of us recognise, or care to acknowledge, and one good way of reminding yourself of this fact is to go walking along disused railways.

Again, the book does not attempt more than a passing glance at the history of the lines explored: since the closure of railways is a subject full of ironies, and I have a certain taste for ironies, I have concentrated mostly on the pioneering stages of these now defunct communication routes. For this reason, the railways are identified by their titles at the time when they were constructed. (A short list of books relating to the lines is supplied for anyone who is interested in walking a line and reading up on it at the same time.) Such technical detail as is included may seem a trifle basic to the mature railway buff: I make no excuse for this short of the fact that I hope the book will be read by those interested in the British landscape as a whole, and in the problems of providing recreational facilities for our large population in that much-exploited terrain, as well as by railway enthusiasts. The book is, then, not so much about the lines as they were, more about the lines as they are now; and what they might be in the future. Indeed, little remains along them now of that intricate and specialised technology with all its strange attendant symbols and curiosly shaped devices except vestigial traces – British Rail, and after them the preservation societies, and after them the private collectors, have seen to that. What old railways 'are now' is parts of the landscape: they seem as much parts in certain places as the long barrows and tumuli of the Bronze Age. What they might be in the future – at least those stretches of them that remain uninterrupted – for walkers, cyclists, equestrians, botanists, ornithologists, poets, gardeners, lovers, and people walking their dogs, as well as for railway buffs, is a subject discussed at length in the concluding section.

The historical detail on some lines has been fleshed out with the recollections of people who once worked them, and of others who were served by them. If you really want to know about the past life of a place or of its one-time railway, ask the locals: that is a recommendation. Without exception the people I spoke to remembered their line – usually very much 'theirs', as if usage gave possession – with affection, no doubt mellowed by the passage of time. Without exception too, everyone I talked to regretted or resented the closures, some with remarkable bitterness after intervals of decades, some rather more theoretically, admitting later that, actually, they had hardly ever used the line themselves. No-one ever said, as they did of road traffic, that the railways were a bloody nuisance and the sooner they got rid of the lot the better. Many felt that since their railway had gone, the place they inhabited had been cut off, despite the roads: and, if they were dependent upon the generally laughable 'alternative transport' said to be available at the time of closure – the infrequent, expensive country bus services – it is by no means difficult to understand their feelings. The first time I asked after railwaymen who had worked the lines I was exploring, the person I spoke to told me dubiously 'I don't think you'll find any, you know. They're all dead now, those old boys.' And elsewhere it was the same: 'They're all gone now,' they said in Suffolk; 'You've arrived a bit late, haven't you?' they asked in Dorset. I began to wonder whether there really were none left: it seemed as if an entire generation of railway workers must have pined to death, killed by the termination of the lines that had been their livelihood. But I persevered, and did in time, from place to place, meet a number of railwaymen from that past age. What they told me brought their lines back to life in a way that no history book could possibly do, no matter whether it had every fact, right down to the dimensions of the last six-wheeled brake van used along the line, tabulated with unerring precision.

The rail-less ways I walked were chosen first and foremost for the places that they pass through. I wanted to find new angles on country already familiar to large numbers of people, be it from footpaths (the Didcot, Newbury and Southampton Railway) or roads (the Bala and Festiniog); lines which went through country quite the opposite, and known to few from any angle (the Midland and South Western Junction Railway outside Swindon, the Cleobury Mortimer and Ditton Priors Light Railway); upland lines and lowland lines, of which the above supply examples; valley lines (the Severn Valley Railway, the Rugby and Stamford as it passes along the Welland valley), and lines running along the water's edge (the Dolgellau Branch from Penmaenpool to Morfa Mawddach); lines which connected the centres of urban areas with the countryside (the Kingswinford Branch at Wolverhampton, the two Teesside lines), and lines running through industrial areas (the Brecon and Merthyr outside Merthyr Tydfil). It was also my intention to examine lines which had been officially reopened as public paths, and to try to form some critical judgement of what had been done: I knew about the Wirral Country Park, and the High Peak Trail in Derbyshire, and three of the four urban railway paths, and went to them accordingly. Later I found that several of the others chosen for other reasons (the Wolverhampton line, the Penmaenpool stretch, sections of line between Lavenham and Sudbury in Suffolk, a section of line at Ironbridge on the Severn Valley Railway and an entire line on the other side of the river from this) had also been developed in similar ways. Finally, I hoped to find lines which retained striking engineering features, as well as mechanical furnishings. In the second of these aims I was largely thwarted: one may well discover viaducts and their remains (at Cefn Coed on the Brecon and Merthyr, for example, or near Barnard Castle in County Durham), or tunnels, or deep rock cuttings, but apart from the unique relics of the Cromford and high Peak Railway, most of the apparatus is now gone and could only be replaced by the labours of preservationists – in which case the lines concerned would no longer be 'disused'.

THE PEDESTRIAN STANDING AT THE DOWN PLATFORM . . .

One facet of railway history that is well worth reflecting upon as you circumnavigate the sheep grazing on the trackbed of some upland station, or heave your way through a scrub and bramble patch on a stretch where little is now left for nature to recolonise, is the fear and loathing which the first arrival of the railways stimulated in some quarters. When Wordsworth heard about the plan to build a railway to Lake Windermere in 1844 he responded characteristically in verse:

> *'Is then no nook of English ground secure*
> *From rash assault?'*

In a protesting letter to the *Morning Post* a part of his conclusion, again in verse, runs:

> *'Now, for your (the mountains') shame, a Power, the Thirst of Gold,*
> *That rules o'er Britain like a baneful star,*
> *Wills that your peace, your beauty, shall be sold,*
> *And clear way made for her triumphal car*
> *Through the beloved retreats your arms enfold!'*

One can appreciate the poet's point of view, especially from this vantage point nearly one and a half centuries later, when it has been repeatedly and resoundingly shown that there *is* no 'nook of English ground secure' from the multiform threats of obliteration by new motorways, airports, open-cast mines, hypermarkets, military installations, and so on, and so forth. If a lot of money can be made, absolutely nothing is safe simply because it is said to be beautiful, or because it has been revered by earlier generations, and it would be sentimentalism to argue against Wordsworth's assessment of the railway pioneers' motivations: the 'Thirst of Gold' was at the very heart of the railway-building phenomenon, as it was at the heart of the industrial revolution itself. For every inspired designer such as Brunel there were a hundred businessmen making out prospectuses telling the citizens of the towns their railways would connect with how they would bring them (or a certain select number of them) prosperity previously undreamed-of, and I doubt if there was one amongst these who cared a twopenny damn about the preservation of the beautiful solitudes of the mountains and river valleys which Romantics such as Wordsworth and Ruskin persisted in their reactionary, old-fashioned way in maintaining were 'sacred'.

On a more mundane level, ordinary people the country over were afraid that the approaching railroads might get routed through their pastures, or their backyards, or worst of all, through their back kitchens. As C. Barman says, the railways 'slashed like a knife through the delicate tissues of a settled rural civilisation. They left their scars on park and copse . . . they brutally amputated every hill on the way.' ('Early British Railways', p. 25.)

In the decade preceding the great period of railway building, there were frequent instances of vigorous opposition, not just to the railways, but to the locomotives that would run along them. In 1831 an indictment was taken out against the Stockton and Darlington Railway Company by local people, for a nuisance originating in their use of locomotive engines: these were described in the evidence as 'those great snorting, roaring and mighty monsters, vomiting fire in all directions', which gave off 'unwholesome and offensive smells, smokes and vapours', and produced 'divers loud explosions, shocks and noises'. (W. W. Tomlinson, 'The North Eastern Railways', p. 382.) During the parliamentary debates preceding the passing of the Great Western Railway Bill in 1835, Counsel claimed that the village of Brompton, 'the most famous of any place in the neighbourhood of London for the salubrity of its air' would be rendered insalubrious ever after, since 'streams of fire would proceed from the locomotive engines'. (C. Hamilton Ellis, 'British Railways History', Vol. I, p. 68.) Of course by no means all such opposition was baseless alarmism. In 1835, for example, an injunction was taken out by a South Shields wine merchant who claimed that vibrations from the nearby engines had caused depreciation of his stock and cracks in his cellar, whilst he and his family had been repeatedly kept awake at night by noise and smoke: he won his case (Tomlinson, p. 383).

It is all the more interesting, then, that in the long run Wordsworth's and Ruskin's aesthetic judgements on the railways were not upheld by the majority. After the first spate of anxiety had passed, and horsemen the country over had learned to keep their steeds in check whenever they were anywhere near a locomotive, people began to appreciate the benefits that the 'snorting monsters' brought them, not just in terms of commerce, but in terms of freedom of movement. The production of acquatints and engravings of railways in the landscape, usually realised in the urbane, conventional styles of the preceding century, became a small derivative industry which helped, or coaxed, individuals into reconceiving these products of new technology in traditional terms. Along the lines the earth's wounds healed over in a very short space of time, and new rock cuttings or embankments colonised by wild flowers often seemed to railway travellers more beautiful than the features that they had usurped. Many people too, acquatints or no acquatints, came to be genuinely inspired by the railway engineering: this did of course take on a somewhat naïvely decorative aspect in the provision of such things as castellated towers at tunnel entrances, but attained to real magnificence in many viaducts and bridges, and was never less than impressive in mountain areas by virtue of the routes – along steep valley sides and over deep gorges – which it succeeded somehow in traversing. If railways were like knives, then they were like very thin knives (in contrast, it is estimated that the land consumed by motorway building today is roughly four times that used by railways, but compare any new major road works) and in country areas at least they were reabsorbed into the landscapes they passed through – as new elements, certainly, but elements hardly more jarring than the ancient roads that wound on either side of them. W. G. Hoskins says in 'The Making of the English Landscape' that today 'we take the railway earthworks and monuments as much for granted as we do the hedges and fields of the enclosure commissioners, or the churches of our medieval forefathers' (p. 267). Even more so do people take railways for granted when they have been written off. Then the blade of the knife turns rusty with vegetation, and given the right conditions and an absence of human intervention, it can grow in as little as twenty-five years into an entirely novel landscape feature: the linear wild wood.

The rate at which a disused line loses its 'railway' look (assuming that it is not redeveloped for other purposes) depends upon what happens at the time of sale. Where a ballast is left down, for example unconsolidated limestone chippings, it is very likely to retain something of its old face for a long time – six years is one estimate – since vegetation has to take root under the ballast and grow up through it; but where the ballast has been sold (typically to local farmers for use as hardcore) the exposed earth trackbed will be quickly taken over, though of course not necessarily by trees. British Rail policy in regard to dismantling is to remove railway furnishings and rails as soon as possible and reuse or sell for scrap through their Supply Department. In the case of rails, the development of the continuous welded rail means that all rails of the old 'bull-headed' type from disused lines can only be reused on other branch lines. Only in rare instances (such as the section of line I walked at Swindon) are the rails left down: this usually means that there is some plan afoot for continued private use of the line.

Dismantling is based on considerations of safety: anything which might conceivably at some time or another drop on the heads of passers-by, or trip them up, or cut them, has to go. But dismantling is also based on considerations of cost: why pay for the maintenance of something you no longer need, it is argued. Hence the early removal of bridges and viaducts, and especially of rail-over-road bridges, which are frequently removed by the highway authorities, who will also dig away the ends of the embankments and smoothe them back out of the way of the road. This procedure, which from a certain, distressingly limited point of view (the point of view adopted by British Rail) is absolutely rational, has been instrumental in robbing literally thousands of miles of disused line of their original function as discrete through routes. Obviously from the point of view of spontaneous railway walking, or any subsequent use of railways as *ways*, this is destructive in the extreme. There are indeed examples of British Rail having assiduously demolished bridges and viaducts before sale only to find that the buyers all along wanted the very structures that they had just spent a lot of money knocking down.

In practical terms, the only method of exploring disused railways at present (apart from the few lengths which have been opened to cyclists and horse riders) is to walk. The theoretical advantages of old railways for conversion to walkers' routes have been noted by several writers: they have easy gradients and no stiles or obstacles, and they can make good paths, particularly for older people. These observations are useful in relation to certain routes, for instance the Bala–Festiniog line, a section of which runs along a very steep valley side where there could be no equivalent footpath even for the toughest hikers, giving magnificent views and the easiest of walking. But there is very often also a related problem. The gentle gradients and lack of contrast on railway lines can be simply boring, and in hills it can be frustrating because you climb without ever reaching a recognisable hilltop, and find yourself going down before you know that you are up. In other places, easy gradients or not, fully disused lines can be difficult terrain. On some stretches you are virtually in need of a machete to hack your way through the undergrowth, and cuttings can get flooded or blocked by dumping. Where a ballast of chippings is left down you need tough ankles, well supported by good boots, or you will get nowhere; and even so walking on such a surface, with the ballast chinking under you like bagfuls of coins, will quickly prove tiring. To relieve monotony where it occurs, I would advise all but the most ardent railway admirers to plan journeys on which they can every so often leave the line and take a look at interesting non-railway features in the surrounding area.

The *feeling* of walking old railways is however, at its best, unique. The landscape has many dimensions, which change according to where you stand, or walk, or sit to see it, and sometimes when you are on a disused railway you will see the landscape as if from a carriage window seat (looking sideways), or even better, as if from the cab of a locomotive (looking forwards). The phrase 'travelling under one's own steam' has particular significance for the railway walker: there are times, when you have had your eye fixed for some time on that sustained vanishing point, always there ahead of you on a clear stretch of track, when it may seem as if you yourself are turning into a somewhat smaller, rather less sturdy kind of locomotive. Always you are headed up and around the next gentle bend; and on, and on. It can become a kind of monomania. There are other times when, in a different mood, you may mistake the sound of a farm machine for that of an oncoming train: the chug of the petrol engine turns into a distant chuffing, and you begin to wonder, was that not the rattle of wheels on short-length rails, echoing under some nearby bridge? But then you look for the rails and find only weeds, or the dumpings from somebody's garden.

If you relax into the role of passenger, you will see how disused railways can retain something of the separateness from the places that they pass through which working lines possess. In towns and industrial zones the view is always of the back-ends of things, of houses, factories, scrapyards and power stations, whilst in the country you will travel through many backwoods areas unknown to road travellers, – but at the same time embankments will raise you up above the fields, or cuttings will take you through the substance of the hills, obscuring everything. The complexities of places tend to be ironed out if you follow such a route, and the effect can be one of alienation; always passing through, but never arriving. Only when the surrounding vegetation has climbed up across the track to meet you will this effect be neutralised – then you will be very much a part!

On disused railways, the past is present, or can seem to be so. At times you may seem to believe that you will alight from the 'train' at the next small town station, and that it will be 1912, say, or 1925 (it does not very much matter which) and horse-drawn carts will be waiting to pick up the empty milk churns, or that an open-topped railway bus will be waiting on the cobbles to carry you to the hotel in the high street. On hot days, on certain stretches of track, you may seem to smell the smoke of locomotives . . . but then you realise that it is simply the ash ballast under your feet, responding to the sun. You will reflect, perhaps, upon the fall of empires, and on that implacable process whereby once-functioning systems produced entirely out of human ingenuity will, given time, disappear from the face of the earth, and the machines and buildings made to support them gradually revert to soil. You may, if you care about railways, gnash your teeth at the ubiquitous ironies that have been generated by the closures; at how, for example, West Bay station at Bridport is now in use as a boat builder's yard, or at the many transformations of track to road, and station site to car park, or at the fact that the line south of Swindon was used for the last time in the construction of the M4, like a man assisting in the erection of his own gallows.

The effect of such reflections on this book is perhaps that it has something of the quality of an elegy. How could it be otherwise? The end of a particular way of getting things done; the end of a phase of transport technology that produced machines some of which, at least, were capable of firing the imagination like creatures out of myth and fable; and the end of the last generation to work those machines when they were needed in society at large – these are the three central facts which anyone exploring disused railways now will repeatedly confront. And the surviving representatives of that last generation are always quick to point to the values that have been, if not absolutely lost, then certainly subsumed into other, and less obvious, and perhaps less appealing forms: the pride in doing the job well, of doing the job a little better than was necessary, the hierarchical structure of employment in which ordinary men could attain to dignity by working with commitment because (for all its faults) the hierarchy was believed in, the very fact of commitment in a job which involved nothing more profound, when you think about it, than getting people and objects from A to B and sometimes back again.

There is elegy too, if that is the right word, in the remains of the lines themselves. Anyone who sees the unwanted viaducts (those that have not been demolished), or stands inside the useless tunnels still penetrating mountains (those that have not been bricked up), will understand this straight away. Anyone who looks at the engravings of John Cooke Bourne with the slightest awareness that the massive, almost titanic labours of the much-exploited navvies and horses portrayed there were *realities,* will travel disused lines with a sense of fabulous, inconsequential waste. What was all that labour for, after all? Surely it justified much more than a single century, or less, of operation? Railway leases were generally taken out for 999 year periods. Surely – even if the railways could not have been kept open – some other transport could have been found for them, since so much planning and work (and destruction of what went before) had gone into laying them out as through routes?

Between the 1st January 1948 (the date of nationalisation) and the end of 1982, British Rail closed 8,144 miles of line in England and Wales. Between 1969, when it was established, and the end of 1982, the British Rail Property Board sold 7,094 miles of this disused track, in lengths varying from many miles to the extent of a private garden, and has negotiations in hand on a further 443 miles. The Countryside Commission Report 'Disused Railways in the Countryside of England and Wales' (1970) estimates that '. . . over the last few years the area of railways falling into disuse annually is roughtly commensurate with the total average land requirements of a new town housing about 80,000 persons' – the only problem being that if a new town were to be built every year to bring this railway land back into use again, it would need to be very long, and very thin. One may not be able to argue with the closures, assessed coldly in terms of profit and loss: so many of the branch lines were not getting the traffic they needed from the areas they served, and stories of services running in their last stages with only railway staff on board are common. But why, why did no-one have the foresight to keep the network intact? Why were the lines not retained as a system of through routes? As I shall argue in the last part of this book, we might well have been able to use them.

A NOTE ON TRESPASS

I must advise anyone thinking of exploring disused railways that are not officially open for public access to obtain permission first from the owner or owners.

Where the land has been sold by British Rail and is in the hands of private individuals, anyone entering can in principle be taken to court by the owners: in this case the trespass, if it is seen to be such, is regarded in law as a civil matter, in other words a legal dispute between individuals.

Where the land remains in the hands of British Rail, even if it is completely disused, it is a criminal offence to enter (under the Railway Regulations Act of 1860 and the British Railways Act of 1965). It is possible for those entering without permission to be fined; fines are lower on disused than on used railways. Permission to walk on disused railway land may be obtained from the British Railways Board, 222 Marylebone Road, London NW1 (01 262 3232).

The way to establish ownership is to write to the Estate Surveyor and Manager in the relevant British Rail Regional Headquarters (located in Bristol, Birmingham, Manchester, York, Glasgow, King's Cross and Victoria), defining clearly which stretch of line you are interested in.

So much for principle. In practice, if you were to follow this advice, you would have to do a lot of letter-writing before you did any walking since the majority of lines are now owned in very short lengths, depending on whose land they pass through. You may therefore find it easier to do the asking of permission as you travel, though my experience as noted on the Cleobury Mortimer and Ditton Priors Light Railway does show that not all owners will be responsive to this approach. Conversely, you may find some who share an interest in railways, and they are much more likely to lean on a gatepost and have a friendly chat than to take you to court if you did happen, by some extraordinary oversight on your part, to be there without permission.

A FOOTNOTE TO THE 1983 EDITION

Whilst I was first working on this book I frequently had in mind the thought that it should by rights be called 'Railway Cycle Rides', awful title as that is. This feeling was very much confirmed by the publication in January 1982 by the Department of Transport of a massive report entitled 'Study of Disused Railways in England and Wales',* which was drawn up by John Grimshaw and Associates, a Bristol-based firm of engineers. This report is all that the Appleton Report was not: it consists of a general survey, a map of the disused lines showing those already converted and those which it proposes for conversion, and a series of 31 separate 'annexes', each of which deals in fine and pragmatically conceived detail with the potential for conversion to shared bike and pedestrian use of one or several stretches of line, all of which are already in the possession of local authorities.

The emphasis in the Study is *primarily* on the benefits of converted railway routes for cyclists, particularly in the case of those leading out of urban areas into countryside, or linking one town with another. One of the Study's findings is that of the 500 miles or so of disused lines already open to the public as paths in England and Wales, the amount originally converted specifically for cyclists adds up to the magnificent total of 6¼ miles! But all the evidence suggests that it is the shared path which will be of most benefit to the public – and that it is the shared path which the public now wants. A pilot conversion of a section of the Midland Railway branch line running between the suburbs of Bath and Bitton in Avon showed that usage of this path, once open, was split roughly 50/50 between cyclists and pedestrians.

It seems, and it is very much to be hoped, that we will now see some real changes. Government attitudes to cyclists have certainly changed, as is shown for example by the publication of the DoT 'Consultation Paper on Cycling' in 1981, and it can only be a matter of time before this percolates through to the local authorities, many of which would have helped the cyclist more in the past, if only the money had been there. For the projects dealt with in the Study, money is now available: the Manpower Services Commission has agreed to sponsor the full 2,000 man-years of work necessary to complete them (a modest amount compared to those called for in larger and more ambitious job-creation programmes), and John Grimshaw has been appointed to supervise and co-ordinate the completion of what he and his team have started. Indeed, even before the Study was published, a number of the conversions proposed by it had already got off the ground. Just under 600 miles of disused railway are proposed for upgrading to paths, and another 180

*Available from HMSO or from Cyclebag, 35 King Street, Bristol B51 4DZ.

miles of route are to be developed along adjoining canal towing paths and bridleways. The Study states, somewhat guardedly, that there could be another 600 miles of line which might in time be usefully converted: John Grimshaw's personal estimate runs at between 1200 and 1800 miles. We may have lost our chance of a comprehensive network based on disused railways; nevertheless it does seem that much remains to be saved. Certainly the development of the Study's existing projects must set the ball rolling in the right direction: the number of successful examples of railway conversions (sometimes incorporating shared use with steam preservation societies) is likely to proliferate in the near future – and examples are exactly what we need.

For this reason I have not attempted to update the list of conversions in the Appendix: any such amended version would itself very quickly go out of date – at least, I hope so! The reader is best advised to get hold of a copy of the Study, and to keep his eye on the lines concerned: he might also benefit in this respect from membership of the Railway Ramblers (see page 283), whose quarterly publication 'Ramblings' occasionally includes details of new schemes, both those projected and those realised. (More detailed appraisals of the Study appear in the March/April 1982 edition of Friends of the Earth's 'Bicycles Bulletin', and in my article 'A Permanent Way for the Bicycle' in the May 1982 edition of 'Bicycle' magazine.)

One further small point. The rhetorical question I posed on page 260 – 'When has any similar move been made by the nationalised British Rail?' – does in fact have an answer, and I owe BR my apologies for not having included it in the first place. The British Rail Property Board has made several attempts in recent years to give away stretches of line and buildings to local authorities for constructive purposes in the general public interest. An example of this is the 'purchase' in 1979 by the Greater Manchester Council of a 2¾-mile stretch of line between Chorlton Junction and Heaton Mersey for a nominal £1, with the intention of converting into a footpath. Efforts have been made, then: but, unfortunately, my argument remains substantially unaltered by this fact. The BRPB has attempted to act constructively only within what is a fundamentally destructive brief. It was this brief, to get rid of disused lines by breaking them up into short lengths, which should have been curtailed from the start.

G.L.J.

RAILWAY · WALKS ·

EXPLORING DISUSED RAILWAYS

PART TWO NEW USES FOR OLD RAILWAYS

In the past thirty years, disused railway land and buildings have been put to a remarkable variety of new uses. In many places the railway formation is no longer to be seen, though it can always be found on either side of the redeveloped length; in others it has been given some new job, but keeps its shape. This section of the book attempts to give a representative, though not comprehensive, picture of the re-employment of redundant lines.

To begin with, some railways have remained railways, in use by industrial organisations either by purchase or lease from British Rail:

The one-time Vale of Neath Railway in the Cynon Valley, Glamorgan, is now owned by the National Coal Board and used for transportation of coal to the Aberaman Phurnacite Plant, in the background. (Another line running through the plant itself, once the Taff Vale Railway, remains in the hands of British Rail for the carriage of coal and silica).

This line, which once ran the length of the Wye Gorge along the Monmouth-Gloucestershire border, remains open southwards from the quarry at Dennel Hill, north of Chepstow, and is still in the ownership of British Rail. The quarry has removed a substantial piece of the hillside here since 1931, when it was opened: ten men and their machines now shift around 2000 tons of ballast per week, which travels to the main line at Chepstow, for use in the maintenance of the surviving railway network.

25

This handsome engine shed at Ashbourne, Derbyshire, is in the process of being made into a factory for Nor'West Textiles.

In other places, railway buildings have been converted to industrial premises .
. . . or industrial buildings have been sited on what was once railway land:

The works for a granite quarry at Arenig, near Pont-Rhyd-y-Fen, Meirionnydd, is sited across the railway which once served it; the station building is now an office.

Storage tanks for a chemical firm sited along a cutting at Lavenham, Suffolk. The works is on the station site, and the station house is now a home for a night watchman.

Old railway lines have been made into sites for pipelines and pylons . . .

Near Hardwick, Teesside.

At Jackfield, near Ironbridge, Salop.

In other places, station sites are used as coal merchants' yards (see the Bala and Festiniog), and the trackbeds themselves may prove useful as haul roads for construction works (the Somerset and Dorset, the Border Counties Railway). Lines may form the bases for new roads, though they are almost always re-engineered:

The South Durham and Lancashire Union at Stainmore Summit, Cumbria. The new re-routing of the A66 on the left covers the trackbed. Two double-track railways could be fitted into the width of land consumed here in the new roadworks alone.

Bridport, Dorset: the line has disappeared under a new town bypass. The hotel name gives a clue to what once stood nearby.

Local councils may take over ex-railway property for their own uses:

The station area at Ironbridge, Salop has been made into a car park. The road at left follows the direction of the old line.

Siting of a skip dump for public use near Dulcote, Somerset.

Another railway site now in the service of roads: Bellingham station, Northumberland has been converted into a depot for the county highways department.

In other places, for example at Bala, Meirionnydd, the railway station has been replaced by a fire station; at Muswell Hill, London (see the Muswell Hill line) a school has taken the station's place.

Railway land has been used for housing, though most frequently (because of the restrictive shape) as an integrated part of larger developments:

It has been used for housing mobile homes:

Cricklade, Wiltshire, viewed from the embankment which once led on to a rail-over-road bridge. The line would have continued where the housing estate now stands.

The Riverside Mobile Home Park, Monmouth. These structures straddle the line of the railway.

Bridgnorth, Salop. The ballast is still visible where walkers keep the brambles back. The new house ahead is at the end of a row built right across the line.

Railway houses have remained occupied, after the lines they were attached to closed . . .

Edington Burtle, Somerset.

The station, Much Wenlock, Salop, now three council houses. A good deal of effort has gone into preserving the external appearance of the building, and floors have been inserted at a point only two thirds of the way up the ground floor windows of the station office, in order to create an extra storey there.

Individual private houses have been built on railway land, and cuttings have been turned into gardens:

A play area made from a cutting at Upton, Oxfordshire. The owner was in two minds about where to fill it in completely _ earth dumping was carried out at the far end but decided that he liked the dip. (It is instructive to note that when he first approached British Rail in order to try to purchase the land, they adamantly, and wrongly, maintained that they did not own it!

The station house, Cleobury Mortimer, Salop. The lawn grows on a few inches of transported soil; underneath this lies solid rock, which had been the foundation of the trackbed here. The owners also built some sleepers into their greenhouse, and loose stone, possibly from the original excavation for the line, is now a part of their rockery.

Private use of old lines can, of course, be unofficial:

Out of sight, out of mind. Dumping at the northern end of the Valley Park, Wolverhampton.

Bonfire on the line near Thorpe by Water, Rutland: the photograph was taken on November the 4th.

One of the commonest views along dead railways: the dumped car here is in use as a hen coop. The station beyond is at Fawley, Herefordshire.

Old railways have proved of use to sportsmen:

The golf course at Bridgnorth: you do not need to be a trained industrial archaeologist to see where the line ran here.

Feeder for pheasants, near Barrowden, Rutland. As well as forming spontaneously into retreats for wildlife, many old lines are used by local landowners as game cover.

An embankment at Alnwick, Northumberland has been made into a running track; at Winchester a section of line has become a small bore rifle range; and another widespread, larely unofficial use of derelict lines is for motorcycle scrambling.

Agricultural uses vary with the country the lines pass through, and also with the physical shape of the railway formations themselves:

Silage clamp near Eastbury, Berkshire.

Reclamation of a cutting near Chilton, Oxfordshire. Cuttings are often purchased by the owners of adjacent land and then simply left as they are since filling them in, along with the removal of fences and provision of a suitable topsoil, can be costly. However if contact is made with building firms, which are prepared to pay high prices to dump their site waste, exactly the opposite can be the case.

Timber yard on the site of Monmouth station.

Private dump in a cutting near East Garston, Berkshire.

This was once a railway cutting, near Lavenham: the 'wall' was the top of a road-over-rail bridge. East Anglian farmers appear to have carried out more total reclamation to date than in any other part of the country, aided by the fact that long stretches of line in East Anglia were at ground level.

The commonest agricultural reuse of old railways is as farm roads (see, as one of several examples, the Cleobury Mortimer and Ditton Priors) in which case no re-engineering is required, though resurfacing is often carried out. In this role the railways have proved invaluable, giving level access where none previously existed. They have also been used for housing new farm buildings, or industrial buildings serving agriculture (a carrot-washing plant at Holme Hale, Norfolk, for instance). They have been used for planting trees as windbreaks, and cuttings especially in hilly areas are sometimes used for feeding stock in winter, since they are sheltered from the weather. Others in areas of impervious rock have been blocked and used as irrigation reservoirs.

41

Last, but by no means least, disused railways have been made back into *used* railways by steam preservation societies. As examples I selected two societies in the same area, one well established, the other not yet operating services.

The Severn Valley Railway Society was formed in 1965, and having been granted a Light Railway Order by the Department of the Environment only after 'considerable difficulties' the Severn Valley Railway began services on a 5-mile section of line south from Bridgnorth, Salop. The length in use has gradually been extended as far as Kidderminster, a distance of nearly 15 miles, though the last two miles leading to an end-on connection with British Rail is being operated only on special occasions until such time as this very useful link can be fully reopened. There is already some use of the line by local people, in addition to the tourists and railway lovers. Is it possible that the society will eventually find itself in the position of supplying a bona fide passenger service to its own area? On one section, at Arley, trackwork and signalling have been recently installed to enable trains to pass there, so that services can now operate on a 40-minute frequency, which gives some indication of the popularity of the line at peak periods.

Railwaymen's holiday. Weekend maintenance on the bogie wheels of loco 2-6-0 LMS Class 5, number 45110, 'RAF Biggin Hill'. This is being carried out by SVR members who during the rest of the week are in the employment of British Rail. The society does, of course, have members in other professions: one of the grimy persons around that day was at certain other times a divorce solicitor.

43

The Telford (Horsehay) Steam Trust may eventually supply to the Ironbridge area what the SVR can no longer provide due to 'development' of the line to the north – a working steam railway. The Trust was formed in 1976 and is currently involved in the restoration of three locomotives; one of these is to become a static exhibit in a part of the Ironbridge Gorge Museum, but the others will be used on the stretch of line running between Horsehay and Lightmoor, with possible extension into Coalbrookdale. A further plan, nothing more than a dream at this stage, is to continue over the river Severn along a stretch of line which serves Ironbridge power station, and then run back along the disused Severn Valley line (for a picture of this stretch see the section on the Severn Valley Railway) to Ironbridge itself.

'Restoration' is a misleadingly easy-sounding word: it requires a somewhat greater physical effort to restore a locomotive to what is usually rather more than its former glory than to restore a piece of porcelain. One HST member had spent all his weekends for several months wire-brushing the rust off a water tank from the inside, a job that had by no means improved his respiration, and as a result of which he also caught a kidney infection. Those who are driven to such acts by love seem simply mad to others whose interests lie elsewhere. Why bother, they say. Who needs those old steam engines? They are no longer important, they have no relevance now. Yet all over the country disused railway lines have been and are being brought back to life, by 'madmen' who will admit to no such thing.

The Horsehay locomotive shed, out of which more than one fully operative loco will eventually emerge. The Adamson-Butterley engineering works is in the background: freight is dispatched along the line at infrequent intervals, and it has been kept open for that purpose. Not far from this rusting track, in 1767 or 1768, the first iron rails ever used were laid to serve the Horshay ironworks.

Loco 0-8-0 G2, LNWR, on the left and members in the Horsehay shed.

47

However, for the casual explorer of disused railways, especially in country areas, it may well seem that along most stretches the lines are not being used for anything at all . . .

RAILWAY WALKS
EXPLORING DISUSED RAILWAYS

PART THREE   EXPLORATIONS

With some exceptions the photographs are arranged in sequence, beginning at one end of each section explored and ending at the other. They show the direction in which I was walking, or side views, except where mentioned in the captions. The numbers of the relevant Ordnance Survey map or maps in the 1:50,000 series are given at the beginning of each section.

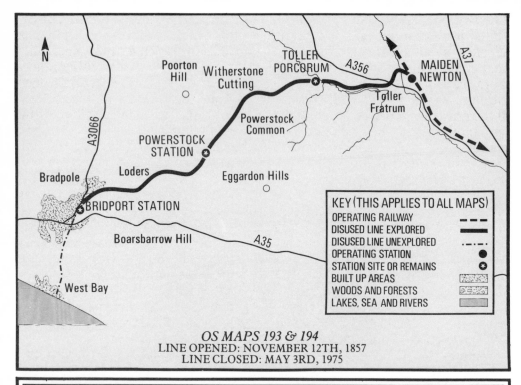

OS MAPS 193 & 194
LINE OPENED: NOVEMBER 12TH, 1857
LINE CLOSED: MAY 3RD, 1975

THE BRIDPORT RAILWAY

FROM MAIDEN NEWTON TO BRIDPORT, DORSET (9 MILES)

16 Oct. 1854

'Sir,

We the undersigned residents of Bridport and its vicinity, deeply interested in the prosperity of the town and its neighbourhood, having carefully read and considered the report . . . on the practicability of the railway from Maiden Newton to Bridport, wish to express our sense of the great importance and advantages of this undertaking . . . and of our hope of your complete success in carrying it through.

We remain, Sir

Yours respectfully . . .'

(Letter to the solicitor handling the legal aspects of the building of the Bridport Railway, signed by the Mayor and 160 other Bridport townsfolk.)

The Bridport Railway was constructed to connect at Maiden Newton with the Wiltshire, Somerset and Weymouth Railway, itself a branch of the Great Western's system. It was intended as a goods and passenger link that would enable Bridport to expand its manufacturing and trading capabilities, and a large part of the directorship consisted of factory owners. Bridport's main industry was and is the manufacture of rope and nets, which until the advent of the railway was dependent on sea transport, whilst the town's hilly environs had made it difficult to reach by road even in good weather. The rope manufacturers were the new railway's biggest customers, but many other local companies benefited from it, including those in villages along the line, though at the best of times the expansion was very modest.

Nor did the town of Bridport itself grow quite so radically as the railway prospectus had forecasted. The branch provided a passenger link with the rest of England and vice versa, but as Bridport was not situated on the Dorset coast, only close to it, it did not prosper as a holiday resort: After the railway was extended to the harbour in 1884 (when the harbour was renamed West Bay) there were plans to build a new resort there which would rival Bournemouth in its grandeur, but nothing more came of this than a single esplanade. The line was however always very useful to local passengers, and even in its last years it was still being ridden by a relatively large number of people: in 1967 an average of a hundred passengers per day was recorded.

For much of its length a pleasant route to walk now, but for the fact that the ballast remains down, the Bridport Railway passes through a fine stretch of western Dorset and is uninterrupted by development or territorial barricades until one approaches Loders, where new housing and a temporary fence suggests that there will be enclosures there. Further west at Bradpole the suburbs of Bridport have obliterated the track, and beyond this all is lost: the site of Bridport station can be detected only by the presence of a couple of sheds in a timber yard, and from here to the terminus at the harbour the railway has become a road.

The exit from Maiden Newton is unusual, passing through a cutting under five closely placed road bridges, but immediately opening out into an embankment smoothing your way up the broad-bottomed Hooke valley. Here, as on the Cleobury Mortimer line, the contrast between the ups and downs and rounds and abouts of the country roads and the easy, imperceptible slope and curve of the railway is striking, and conducive to smugness, or boredom, in the railway walker, depending on his mood. On the left here, and well worth a detour, Toller Fratrum, a monkish outpost of Forde Abbey, sits high on a knoll, its fine old farmhouse set off against a rounded wood-clump.

Beyond Toller Porcorum, where the level crossing has turned into a meadow, you climb through rough, infertile-looking fields towards Witherstone Cutting, 'the bug-bear of the Bridport Railway Company and the thief of the shareholders', as the *Bridport News* called it back in 1858, since during the engineering of the line it was repeatedly the site of troublesome landslips.

This stretch of the line could serve as a textbook example of the aesthetic problems posed by disused railways for the walker, which for the cyclist wanting to get from A to B are almost certainly offset by the advantages of easy gradients – given that the surface is cyclable. In the first place you climb the hill but you do not know you climb the hill: you are descending before you realise that you have reached the highest point, and the fact that the highest point is in a cutting means that there is no long view such as you could experience from the hills on either side. In the second place the stretch down to Powerstock, passing through the nature reserve of Powerstock Common, *should* have long views. But these are a rarity because the track has been enclosed on both sides by trees and shrubs. The effect is one of absolute separation: you pass through the area, which is as deep into backwoods country as you could hope to go, but remain always shut off from it. Glimpses of thatch and rolling chalk hills with scrub on their steep slopes serve to remind you that you are in Darzet; but otherwise it would be necessary to have the skills of a botanist in order to deduce the country either side from the evidence of railway flora. In this context the Witherstone Cutting would seem to be a very promising site, a part of which the Dorset Naturalists' Trust is hoping eventually to control (the existing nature reserve, accessible from the line, has been seriously encroached upon by deadly Forestry Commission conifer plantation).

At Loders I met a local, walking his dog. He told me how he used to sit on the hill above the village and watch the trains go by, and of the pleasure the sight had always given him. He told me that you could get a good angle from up there, to take a photograph, if there was a train coming. However, at the other end at Maiden Newton one of the men who had ridden the line and also worked on taking up the rails when it was closed, reflected 'You know, I can't remember what it was like, now . . .'

(*Above*) *Parting of ways. Right branch by train for Yeovil and beyond. Left branch by foot for Bridport. In practice however this is not a good place to join the old line, as one would be trespassing on British Rail property, at £200 a time.*

(*Left*) *Old fence post on the embankment. The figure 4 is a mark indicating the distance in chains from the junction with the Yeovil line. The markings were made during the lifting of the rails to give clear divisions when it came to selling off the land in sections, and similar figures (in miles and chains) can be seen in many other places.*

(Above) Concrete tank traps installed during the second World War. For some reason British Rail omitted to remove them for sale or reuse elsewhere. The embankment would have functioned as a line of resistance in the event of an attack on the south coast. Near Maiden Newton.

(Right) A high embankment leading to a bridge over the river Frome.

(Above) The branch as it
approaches Toller Porcorum
(not a pig in sight on the day I
was there). River Hooke in the
foreground.

(Far left) Toller Porcorum
station, a typical small Great
Western station, wood with a
brick base. The gents here is
made of cast iron.

(Left) Platform entrance,
Toller Porcorum. Grass on the
platform, grass on the track,
yet . . . This is one of those
places where you can find
yourself wondering whether, if
you waited long enough, a
train might not yet come rolling
in.

(Right) Descending the hill to Powerstock station; a now rare view of Poorton Hill which passengers sitting on the right hand side of the carriage would once have enjoyed.

(Right) Powerstock was called Poorstock until the railway arrived, after which it was given a name more fitting to a settlement connected by the permanent way.

(Right) Farm crossing gate by Powerstock. The unnecessary wrought-iron curves give that little decorative touch so conspicuously lacking in most modern design.

(Above) 'Dreaded Loders Bank', as one poet of the Bridport Railway called it. The gradient of 1 in 75 made it necessary for goods trains not fitted with vacuum brakes to stop before the downhill journey so that a number of wheels on the wagons could be pinned down.

(Left) Ganger's hut, now gang hut. It is constructed out of old sleepers.

(Right) View of Loders from the railway . . .

(Below) . . . but what railway? This stretch has been completely reclaimed. The line ran along the trees at the left. Looking back towards Toller Porcorum.

...BLIC NOTICE

...SSENGER SERVICE

...DEN NEWTON - BRIDPORT

...Secretary of State for the Environment has given his consent to the withdrawal ...e railway passenger service between Maiden Newton and Bridport on condition ...he service is not withdrawn before 5 May 1975. The consent was conveyed in ...r dated 30 December 1974, addressed to the British Railways Board, a copy ...of which is reproduced hereunder :-

Department of the Environment
2 Marsham Street London SW1

MAIDEN NEWTON — BRIDPORT RAIL CLOSURE PROPOSAL.

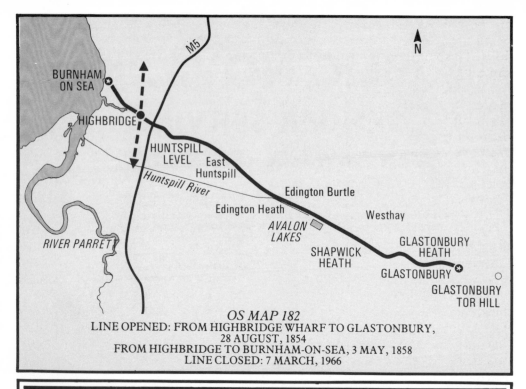

OS MAP 182
LINE OPENED: FROM HIGHBRIDGE WHARF TO GLASTONBURY,
28 AUGUST, 1854
FROM HIGHBRIDGE TO BURNHAM-ON-SEA, 3 MAY, 1858
LINE CLOSED: 7 MARCH, 1966

THE SOMERSET AND DORSET JOINT RAILWAY

FROM BURNHAM-ON-SEA TO GLASTONBURY, SOMERSET (13½ MILES)

The Somerset and Dorset began as two separate railways of different gauges, the northern half being initially a broad-gauge line. The section between Highbridge Wharf and Glastonbury was the first to be opened, by the Somerset Central Railway Company, and served to connect Glastonbury with the harbour at Highbridge, where amongst other goods Caerphilly cheese made in Somerset was shipped to Wales. The line was constructed economically along the route of the Glastonbury Canal, which was closed for the purpose. The extension to Burnham enabled trains to run out on to a 900-foot-long pier built with the intention of promoting a rail-fed shipping link with Wales for passenger traffic. The Dorset Central Railway, meantime, was planning to meet the Somerset Central from the south, and amalgamation of the two companies occurred in 1862: trains could then run from Burnham on the north coast to Poole on the south coast, the last part of the journey being over the rails of the London and South Western line from the metropolis. Despite the connection of Bristol and English channels, however, the shipping link at Burnham did not prosper.

The Somerset and Dorset provided a convenient route whereby holiday-makers could get from the Midlands to Bournemouth, which expanded partly as a result of it, and amongst other goods the line carried Midlands beer from Burton-on-Trent, helping to precipitate the closure of many south western breweries. Coal was the major freight transported, mainly to the south from the north Somerset coalfield. Passenger use was heavier along the line's northern half, but in its latter years services were at best – as David St John Thomas observes – 'miserably slow, and at worst indescribable'. ('Regional History of the Railways', Vol. I, p. 199.)

The Burnham end of the line is now exceedingly unexciting (why anyone should want to go to Burnham, a more than gone-to-seed holiday resort, I cannot imagine, unless it be of necessity – to attend a funeral of an aged relative, for example): though the 900-foot-long pier remains, for amusement purposes. The line there may be used for new road access to the town centre; the station is gone, but the site is not yet redeveloped. A mile and a half east of East Huntspill a bridge has been demolished, so anyone wishing to explore this part of the line might be best advised to start a mile further to the east of this point. The railway crosses the variously named moors and heaths of the Sedgemoor district towards Glastonbury in an almost uninterrupted straight line, and has either been converted into farm roads or forms the central access route for the 'Avalon Lakes' scheme and, until this scheme matures, is used for peat extraction haulage. It is only distinguishable as a railway at road crossings, where in several places there are crossing-keepers' houses, level crossing gates and posts, or bumps in the tarmac indicating the presence of sleepers underneath. This is functional, dead flat country created by the draining of marshland, though with areas of small fields and twisted willows remaining, especially towards Glastonbury. The peat cutting is a major industry and the peat 'harvest' can be seen in places as rows of conical piles of brown blocks. The line runs along an embankment only slightly higher than the fields and heathlands either side of it, and is accompanied by drainage channels along several sections.

Landscapes do not remain static, they are in a permanent state of mutation: the coming and going of the railway across Sedgemoor was just one element in its evolution. So, just as the Glastonbury Canal pre-deceased the railway in order that the railway should be made, the old line is now being used to the west of the Westhay road crossing in the excavation of a huge hole from the sticky clay which underlies the peat there. This is the beginning of a lagoon for Wessex Water Authority's still tentative scheme to construct nine square-edged reservoirs ('Avalon Lakes' sounds rather more lyrical than the probable result) over the next 10 to 20 years. Full development waits upon the completion of peat extraction from the area. No clear policy on recreation has been formulated, short of mapping possible areas for recreational use. It would have been a good idea in any plan incorporating public access to use the line to Glastonbury as a footpath/bridleway linking the town and 'lakes'– unfortunately, this is not a part of the projected plan. Yet the line within sight of Glastonbury makes a fine walk. With the Tor always before you, capped mysteriously by its ruined church, this is one of those distinctive routes which reminds you at every stage that you are getting somewhere. If your imagination is fired by Malory, then the railway is as good a way as any to approach the Isle of Avalon, and the burial place of King Arthur. How strange it is that no footpath link is planned between the Isle of Avalon and the Avalon Lakes, even when one exists there (but for one short section that has been ploughed) ready made in the form of a railway.

The station at Glastonbury is a melancholy ruin, as melancholy as any I have visited. I arrived there just before sundown, when the timber business which occupies the station yard was not operating. The station buildings are largely intact, but most are not in use for anything. The platforms have so far resisted weeds, and look almost as if they are being kept clear by the pacing feet of railway passengers. I waited, but I did not see any. In this desolate place it seemed as though the entire town of Glastonbury beyond might have been similarly abandoned – written off by Dr. Beeching and his committee at the same time as the railway itself, because it did not pay. A local reminisced about the train outings to Burnham that he had gone on when he was at school: in those days, perhaps thirty years ago, a day return had been a shilling. As he talked I noticed that his description – or the way he spoke – called up a real sense of liberation: going off by train, then, was really something. I wonder if he feels the same now when he piles his family into the car and drives down to some overcrowded tarmac car park by the sea?

(A six-mile stretch of the Somerset and Dorset at its southern end, between Blandford Forum and Sturminster Marshall, is now projected for conversion to a bridleway.)

Remains of Burnham station, facing west.

(Below) Line becomes road, Burnham: the railway would have curved round from the bushes at the left.

(Top right) The portrait is of Tom Mogg, one-time crossing keeper at Edington Burtle. I was told that it was a not uncommon occurrence for motorists to have to haul Mr Mogg out of the bar in order to get the gates open. The pub is being renamed the Tom Mogg Inn.

(Above) Edington Burtle

South Drain and railway, south of Edington Burtle. The railway is discernible on the left as a track leading to an opening in a fence. The also disused Bridgwater branch runs from a point ¼ mile west.

(Right) Drainage channel running parallel to the line on its north side, near Westhay.

(Below) Work in progress on the Avalon Lakes scheme. Westhay, facing west.

(Left) Westhay: old ramp for herding cattle into waggons. The rubble remains of a crossing-keeper's house, with a gate to an overgrown path still intact, lie on the other side of the line.

(Below) The 'spine' road-to-be of the Avalon Lakes, near Westhay. There will be stretches of water on either side of the line here, if the plan is carried through.

(*Top*) *Road traffic takes priority: remains of level crossing on Glastonbury Heath, the Tor in the distance. Ahead, the railway is barely perceptible, a grassed bank with a good gravelled farm road behind it.*

(*Above & right*) *Glastonbury station.*

(*Over*) *Shunting wheel, Glastonbury station yard. This acted as a runner for a horse-pulled tow rope and was used for moving single wagons.*

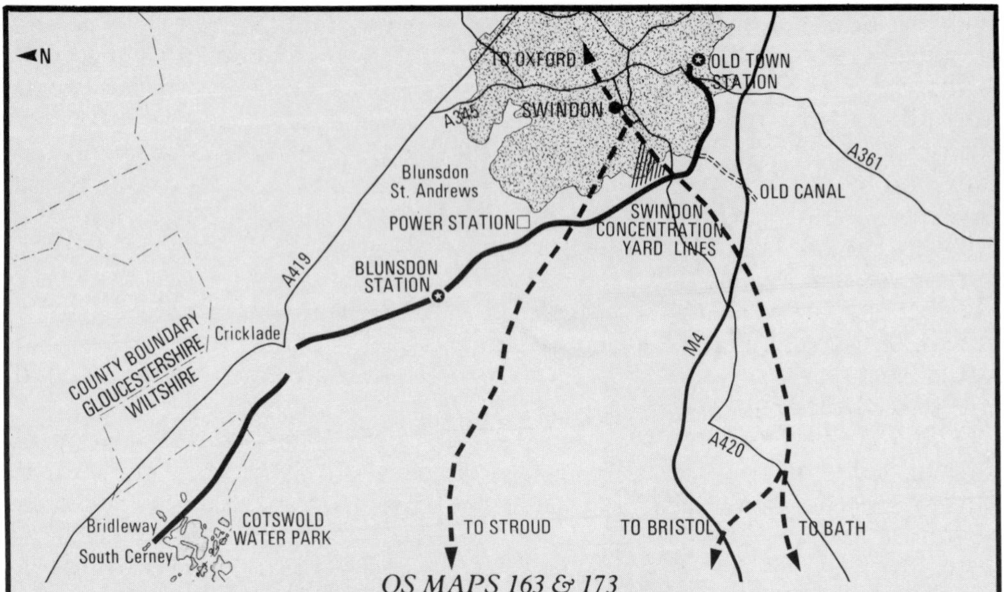
N
TO OXFORD
OLD TOWN STATION
SWINDON
A345
A361
Blunsdon St. Andrews
OLD CANAL
POWER STATION
SWINDON CONCENTRATION YARD LINES
A419
BLUNSDON STATION
COUNTY BOUNDARY
GLOUCESTERSHIRE
WILTSHIRE
Cricklade
M4
A420
Bridleway
COTSWOLD WATER PARK
South Cerney
TO STROUD
TO BRISTOL
TO BATH

OS MAPS 163 & 173

LINE OPENED: FROM SWINDON TO ANDOVER (RED POST JUNCTION), 1882 AND 1883

LINE CLOSED: TO PASSENGERS, 11 SEPTEMBER, 1961

THE MIDLAND AND SOUTH WESTERN JUNCTION RAILWAY

FROM SWINDON OLD TOWN STATION, WILTSHIRE
TO SOUTH CERNEY, GLOUCESTERSHIRE (11½ MILES)

Like the Didcot, Newbury and Southampton Railway, the M&SWJR created a roughly north–south link between the Midlands and beyond with Southampton. The operating company was formed by the amalgamation of two others, the Swindon, Marlborough and Andover Railway Company which built the line south from Swindon, and the Swindon and Cheltenham Extension Company, which built the rest. The railway's title after amalgamation is descriptive – like all early railway titles – of what it could do in its completed state, in this case link the Midland Railway at Cheltenham with the London and South Western Railway at Andover.

There was little local traffic, and the first few years proved difficult, until in November 1892 the M&SWJR was able for the first time to exercise its running powers into Southampton along the existing London and South

Western line: this evidently came about as a result of the company having obtained a new manager, Sam Fay, from L&SW, who had remained on good terms with his old employers. From 1894 passenger trains as well as goods were allowed along the L&SW rails, and the M&SWJR began to operate very efficiently under Fay's skilful timetabling. A major source of income then came in the form of emigrants from the northern cities, Bradford, Leeds and Liverpool, who were leaving from Southampton for the Dominions. Between the wars the line's function as a through north–south route declined, though during them it was in constant use to serve military camps set up on the Marlborough Downs and Salisbury Plain. The railway did indeed grow a 2½ mile branch from Ludgershall, built by the War Office in 1900, which served a permanent military camp at Tidworth on the Salisbury Plain: this remained in use until 1963.

The first impression I had of the line as it runs around Swindon was one of unqualified neglect, but I subsequently discovered that there are many plans for the line on many separate drawing-boards, some of which are already beginning to be realised. Even since I took these photographs, the rails have been lifted. The Old Town Station site, a broad area of some 80 yards in width, is to be used for industrial and residential developments; between the Old Canal and the A420 there may be a road construction scheme, and a timber company will be excavating the embankment to extend its premises; north of the A420 another road construction scheme is already under way, and either side of this industrial developments are projected. Of the section of line between the Old Town station and Moredon power station, only the stretch between the Old Canal and the A361 seems likely to remain walkable, as a council-maintained footpath. Anyone wishing to see the line here in anything like its original shape should waste no time: it will soon be either transformed, or inaccessible.

North of the power station site, too, the dereliction will probably only be temporary, though no railway walker is likely to complain at the intended change back into a steam railway, as a result of the initiative of the recently-formed Swindon and Cricklade Railway Society. This society hopes to relay the track along a one-mile stretch north of the (bridgeless) crossing of the River Ray, at the same time rebuilding the station at Blunsdon, and then gradually to extend in either direction until the full 4½ miles from the power station site to Cricklade is once more a working railway. When that happens the marksmen of Swindon and the dog-walkers of Cricklade will have to look for other places to amuse themselves.

North of Cricklade the line leaves Wiltshire and enters Gloucestershire, passing through the Cotswold Water Park, a new recreation area made out of a vast expanse of disused gravel pits (not all are yet disused). Here the planning is actively geared to public access: one section of the railway adjacent to the largest ponds is already a footpath, and it is intended to convert the line to a path southwards to Cricklade and northwards to Cirencester. (At present part of the southern section is a very unpretty gravel haul route). The Water Park is designated as a Grade One Wetland Habitat, and accordingly visitors are not allowed to trample everywhere. But even so the park is at present an unexciting place: a machine-made landscape where people arrive in machines to play around on the biggest expanses of water in yet other, even noisier machines. It could be beautiful, of course, in forty years, especially if we managed to get rid of the machines. In the meantime there is much more contemplative peace on the old railway before you get to this 'park' than when you arrive.

(*Above*) *End of the line, beyond Swindon Old Town station. Landscaping, completed in 1973, of what was an embankment carrying the line southwards towards Marlborough. Beyond this lies a large new road roundabout.*

(*Over*) *Dead and live railways. The Swindon-Gloucester line is seen here from the north.*

(*Top*) *Expressions of varying faiths. Beyond the 'Jesus Loves' graffito a page out of Isaiah was lying on a sleeper.*

(*Above*) *Underpass to the A361, looking towards the Old Town station site.*

(*Above*) '*A wine-maker's paradise, this,' one rambler observed. I looked for the damsons he told me about, but with no luck. Blackberries, however, grow in profusion. There are many paths across waste ground to this point (½ mile north of the crossing with the main line) from nearby housing estates.*

(Left) 'Unofficial recreational use': air-gun practise with Coke cans as targets. 'Lots of people come down here,' the father told me. 'Nobody will bother you here.'

(Left) The range, with Moredon power station in the background. The power station is also redundant and in the course of being dismantled: a section of line south of this point is retained by British Rail in case, one day, someone decides the power station should be rebuilt, in which case the line will be modified to form a link with the Swindon-Gloucester main line, ¼ mile to the south.

(Top) Cutting by the power station.

(Far right) Half a mile north of the power station. The rails ended a hundred yards to the left.

(Right) Cricklade from the south. The railway is a footpath by common usage, and I met several people walking here. The massive bramble bushes appeared to have been cut back: 'I know somebody drove a Land Rover up here the other week for a bet,' one passer-by told me, 'so that might've helped to keep them down.' The embankment provides high views over the flat country, but is likely to be absorbed in time into the Swindon and Cricklade Railway Society scheme.

(Far right) Old road-over-rail bridge next to which the new spine road of the Cotswold Water Park now runs. This striking construction (there are other surviving examples along the line) is to be preserved as the centrepiece of a car park serving a circular bridleway round the water park, a part of which will be formed by the old line.

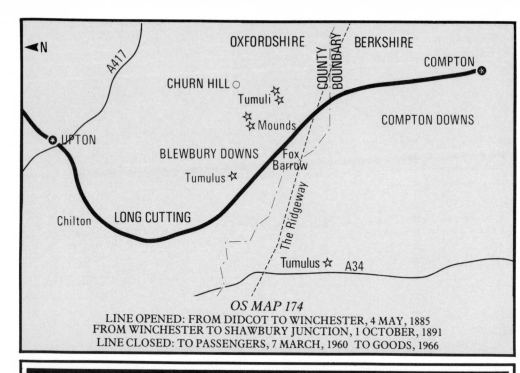

OXFORDSHIRE | BERKSHIRE

◄N

A417

COMPTON

CHURN HILL ○

Tumuli ☆
☆

☆
☆ Mounds

COUNTY BOUNDARY

COMPTON DOWNS

◉ UPTON

BLEWBURY DOWNS

Fox
Barrow

Tumulus ☆

The Ridgeway

Chilton   LONG CUTTING

Tumulus ☆   A34

OS MAP 174

LINE OPENED: FROM DIDCOT TO WINCHESTER, 4 MAY, 1885
FROM WINCHESTER TO SHAWBURY JUNCTION, 1 OCTOBER, 1891
LINE CLOSED: TO PASSENGERS, 7 MARCH, 1960 TO GOODS, 1966

THE DIDCOT, NEWBURY AND SOUTHAMPTON JUNCTION RAILWAY

FROM UPTON, OXFORDSHIRE TO COMPTON, BERKSHIRE (5½ MILES)

'Of course the services are a bit erratic now they've taken the rails up,' one local observed to me dryly, 'but they're not much worse than before.' The early history of the DN&SJR supplies a classic example of competitive overreaching by a small railway company with delusions of grandeur – quite literally overreaching, since several miles of line were constructed which proved in the end to be absolutely unnecessary. The line was at first planned unpretentiously as a useful north–south link between the Great Western line at Didcot and the London and South Western line to Southampton, which it was to join near Micheldever in Hampshire. But the people of Southampton, opposed to development there by the L&SWR, sent a deputation to promise support to the DN&SJR, who accordingly decided that independent entry to Southampton and nothing less must be their goal. The Micheldever link was forgotten, and a diversionary proposition from the L&SWR to make a similar link with the London to Salisbury line at Whitchurch in Hampshire was turned down. Powers were obtained for a direct route into Southampton in 1882, but since very little hard cash had been forthcoming from the good citizens of Southampton, despite their having held a torchlight procession to celebrate the incorporation of the DN&SJR, the company was forced to modify its aims. What it did, against the advice of consultant J. Staats Forbes, 'that noted resuscitator of moribund railways' as H. P. White calls him ('Regional History' II, p. 143), was to build a station in a back street in Winchester, which the line had reached by 1890, and open services in 1891 to virtually no traffic whatever.

As the services lost money the directors quarrelled amongst themselves. Some persevered in their dream of an independent route to Southampton, but Southampton was still a long way away. Eventually, having no further money to invest, the company capitulated to the L&SWR and ran their line a further three miles south, finally making the junction with the L&SW line to Southampton which had originally been planned for Micheldever, having added another twelve unnecessary miles to their route to achieve the same thing. The L&SWR, by now not at all well disposed towards the company, did not grant them running powers over their line, which they would almost certainly have done in the first place, and the Mecca of Southampton remained beyond their grasp. Even in later years, though the line did form a more direct north–south link between Birmingham and Southampton, it never competed with the route via Basingstoke, either for passengers or freight.

The section of the DN&SJR which I walked is one stretch of line where it would be difficult to justify conversion to a path on the grounds of inadequate access elsewhere in the area, since it runs through an expanse of country better served than most by bridleways, trackways and public paths. The cutting illustrated has a path running directly along its southeastern side for about a mile. My entry to it (with permission granted!) was through somebody's back garden (picture p. 39), and two hundred yards further I found my way barred by a stout wire fence and a 'no admittance' sign which were, I was told, erected to prevent illicit use of the track by motorcycle scramblers. Half a mile on I discovered a section almost completely blocked by infilling with earth and rubble (picture p. 44), and another hundred-yard section was, in mid-summer, inches deep in rank-smelling flood water, and very muddy where it was not flooded, since the ballast had been removed.

Despite all this, though, the line here has many rewards. In the first place the cutting runs through chalk hills, and along one stretch the exposed rock surfaces have weathered sufficiently to have deposited small-scale screes of white rubble, the likes of which had caused the track to be realigned on occasions when the railway was working. There is also a profusion of chalk-dwelling plantlife which would be difficult to match along the trackways, especially the overworked Ridgeway, up on the hill: and along one piece of embankment near Upton I found carpets of tuberous vetchling, a kind of wild sweet pea, spreading in a fantasy of cerise-pink as if nothing could stop it, whilst clearly the cutting sides were very soon going to be blued-over with cornflowers. I also stumbled across a dumped Morris Minor, already looking more like a bramble bush than a manufactured thing, which had a freshwater pond formed in its deeply indented roof. Such discoveries, and the lofty ruminations on the vanity of human affairs which they inevitably stimulate, are worth the trouble of a few obstacles.

The DN&SJR track does in fact provide an intriguing new entrance to the area of Oxfordshire/Berkshire downland known as Blewbury Down. With Didcot power station at your back, and Harwell Atomic Energy Research Establishment not more than a mile to your right, this deep, curving cutting is a world to itself in which, immediately you have entered it, both of these twentieth century manifestations become simply inconceivable. Cuttings can indeed be boring to walk along, but this lengthy cutting has become an enclosed, unplanned nature reserve, complete as an experience in itself. When you emerge on to the rolling expanses of Blewbury Down the line is level with the fields, and in some places serves as a farm road. Here, as when crossing moorland, the old railway is still a platform of civilisation from which to look out on to the 'barbaric' downs with their tumuli and barrows, replete with ancientness despite the intensity of arable cultivation. A place to hurry through, it seems from the railway: especially here will you see the landscape as if from the windows of a train, and walk briskly on towards those apparently isolated pockets of civilisation in the south, at Crompton and Newbury.

(Top right) Goods shed, Upton.

(Right) This ring, on the goods shed at Upton, could have been used for pulling a single wagon, using man- or horse-power.

(Far right) Old footpath to the platform at Upton. The station house is still occupied.

(Top right) Steeply angled farm bridge, west of Chilton.

(Right) The cutting west of Chilton, view to the north.

94

(Above) The cutting west of Chilton, view to the south.

(Over) On Blewbury Down.

(*Top*) *Halt near Lower Chance Farm.*

(*Left*) *Blewbury Down.*

(*Above*) *Track-over-rail bridge, which carries the Ridgeway Path across the line. The county boundary follows the path at this point, so the view is of Berkshire, from Oxfordshire.*

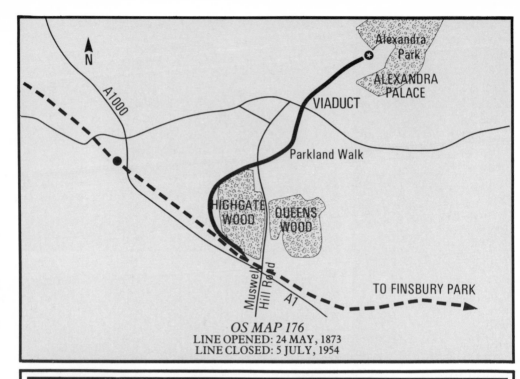

OS MAP 176
LINE OPENED: 24 MAY, 1873
LINE CLOSED: 5 JULY, 1954

THE MUSWELL HILL RAILWAY

FROM HIGHGATE WOOD TO ALEXANDRA PALACE, LONDON: THE PARKLAND WALK (1¼ MILES)

This branch line, which was one of the shortest in the country, was constructed at the same time as the Alexandra Palace with the sole intention of transporting the Palace's expected visitors: at the time Muswell Hill was just a hill, and there was not a single village along the route. The branch opened to passengers on the same day as the Palace. At the start it did fantastically good business; trains and stations must have been full to overflowing since in the first sixteen days the line carried 99,000 people up to the new pleasure dome – but then, on 9th June, the Palace was gutted by fire and the branch had to shut its ticket windows until rebuilding was completed. The fortunes of railway and Palace continued to be inextricably linked: between 1875 and 1898 the Palace was closed seven times, and so was the railway. It was taken over by Great Northern in 1911.

Since closure the branch has been built upon in several places, which is hardly surprising considering the demands for building land in London, though nonetheless a pity. However, the continuity of the route has been for the most part maintained by the insertion of footpaths along or round all new constructions, so that it is now possible to walk from Highgate Wood to Alexandra Palace without using motor roads. A further plan, also under the London Borough of Haringey, is to provide a connection along the old Highgate to Finsbury Park line, which will enable people to walk from Highgate Wood to Finsbury Park itself, thus linking two green 'lungs' in an otherwise completely urbanised area. I must note, however, that the scheme for conversion of this line came about despite, rather than because of, the council. It was necessary for a number of local residents' and conservation groups to do battle with Haringey at a public enquiry in order to prevent them from allowing more housing here – the battle is now won.

Design and management along the section between Muswell Hill Road and Muswell Hill (officially opened as the Parkland Walk in 1974) has produced a largely pleasant informal route. The vegetation has regenerated since the line closed and birch trees have quickly spread, some even growing along the viaduct across St. James' Lane: these give a basic attractiveness to which it will not be difficult to add with further indigenous planting. Wild daffodils and bluebells have been planted, and what is known as a 'conservation seed mix' has also been used: this contains the seeds of many wild flowers, including the seeds of plants considered as weeds in other places. Some more mature trees had evidently been allowed to grow around the backs of the gardens of houses at the top of one embankment even while the line was operating, and these are a great asset now. The resurfacing has been done using a fawn gravel (known in the trade as " 'hoggin-a' clay-bound gravel") which matches well with birch bark, and makes a perfectly adequate ride for cyclists, who are permitted. On top of this the seating is nicely done, using thick logs sawn from end to end to produce half-cylinders themselves supported on further logs, and reinforcements to the path edge have also been made using stakes driven deep into the ground, with just a few inches protruding solidly. When I was there the path was also largely litter-free. All of this goes to show that small budgets (the approximate cost was £17,000, including some restoration of the viaduct, which is now the council's responsibility but is not expected to be a great liability in the future) can be deployed well if a little care, and a little taste, is used; though, naturally, that should not be made an excuse to keep such budgets small.

(Above) Highgate Wood from the line, which is rapidly becoming a part of the wood. Remains of a fence and a 'no trespassing' notice mark the old boundary. Although the line is almost as lovely as the wood, people fling newspapers and Heineken cans off a footbridge passing over it, and local gardeners dump compost on it. Between this and the Parkland Walk a section of cutting is used to house electricity transformers, a school, and a neat redbrick housing estate.

(Above) High embankment (giving almost spectacular views of hills covered with terraced houses) and cat.

(Left) Path users, with new tree growth in rear.

(Far left) The Parkland Walk, east of Muswell Hill Road: the birch trees have grown since the line was closed. Nearby a garden centre is crammed into a narrow strip on top of the embankment.

(Right) St. James' Lane viaduct: the space under every arch has been filled with small buildings housing light engineering works, window-manufacturers, garages. The city came up the hill and surrounded the viaduct, even to the extent of flowing into the spaces between its supports.

(Below) Unpleasant end to the Parkland Walk. Why can't the bin be screened? Why the deadly concrete screening, which is also impossible to paint over once the scrawlers have been at it?

(Below right) From the viaduct east of St. James' Lane. The backs of other people's houses . . .

(Left) Muswell Hill Primary School and playing field, sited across the route of the old line. There is still a path here, diverted round the school into Alexandra Park. The place where I stood to take the picture is part of the park but is reserved for the school on games afternoons. Looking west.

(Left) Reverse positioning to the above. The Ally Pally rears beyond the fence of the park staff yard, again sited across the line.

(Below left) Alexandra Palace Station, and the end of the line that was. The derelict station matches the Palace in the use of yellow brick and rounded arches, but is otherwise much more formally pleasing than that awesomely dreadful structure. The steps up which they flooded in their thousands in 1873 stand to the left of the station, fenced off and unused. Perhaps the ultimate irony that I encountered on any line is that here, a few hundred yards back along the route, the British Railways Research Department is sited. Evidently they do not research into methods of resuscitating disused railways – such as, for example, the Muswell Hill Railway – in this department.

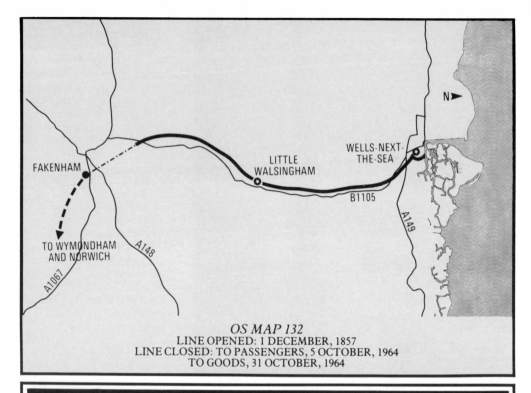

OS MAP 132
LINE OPENED: 1 DECEMBER, 1857
LINE CLOSED: TO PASSENGERS, 5 OCTOBER, 1964
TO GOODS, 31 OCTOBER, 1964

THE WELLS AND FAKENHAM RAILWAY

FROM FAKENHAM TO WELLS-NEXT-THE-SEA, NORFOLK (9½ MILES)

At the time the railway was built, Wells-next-the-Sea was a port of some value to its area, at which coal was imported and farm produce exported, but it was currently in decline since the muddy inlet to its quayside kept out the more modern, larger ships. A series of railways was planned for Wells and two of these were built, the first linking it with Fakenham, the second with Heacham on the west coast of Norfolk and thus with King's Lynn. Despite the arrival of the W&FR, however, the port continued in decline until in 1862 the railway was incorporated into the Great Eastern system, after which it became part of an important north-south route through East Anglia, the main purpose of which was to supply London's markets with produce. When the West Norfolk Junction Railway arrived from Heacham with its link to King's Lynn in 1866, Wells station became a busy terminal for both lines, and for the short harbour branch which had been built in 1860. This was a big station for such a small town, and had an animal-feed mill situated next to it. Amongst other produce, shellfish was transported to London in dripping sacks, and R. S. Joby ('Forgotten Railways: East Anglia', p, 45) records that when the change-over to diesel came about this leakage caused frequent breakdowns because of chemical action on working parts – with the steam trains this had never been a problem.

The other station on the Wells and Fakenham Railway to grow in impor-tance, though not till the 1930's, was Walsingham. After a local woman had a vision of the Virgin Mary in 1061, this village became, along with Lourdes and Santiago de Compostela, one of the main centres of medieval pilgrimage. A twentieth century revival of interest in the place was stimulated by the activities of a very high church Anglican movement centred there, one visible result of which is a shrine church more baroque than many Spanish cathedrals. Catholics have their own separate shrine in a 'slipper chapel' outside the village (this was where medieval pilgrims would remove their foot-covering and pray before walking barefoot over the remaining mile of holy ground): when the railway was running, trains would sometimes stop here to allow pilgrims to disembark. Special trains were run from the Midlands and elsewhere for the most important holy days.

I began to explore to the south of Fakenham, where the Great Eastern line is still in use for goods traffic. Along it I met a permanent way engineer who appeared to be keeping the whole length operational single-handed. I walked down the track with him as far as the crossing with the disused Lynn and Fakenham Railway (which is well worth investigation); unlike me he habitually walked on the sleepers, his pace perfectly adapted to the short stretch. He told me how he regretted the fall in the standards of line maintenance and the fact that here, because of the minimal traffic it receives, the line is barely maintained – the ballast is no longer level, many of the sleepers are rotting – and reminisced about the days when they used to have competitions, with a couple of pounds as a prize, for the best-kept stretch of line. It was not just the station staff, then, with their flower-beds and their fresh paint, who took pride in their work. (On another trip the stationmaster at Driffield in Humberside told me of the times they used to rig up ploughs in order to turn over the earth along embankments there which are now mostly reafforested.)

The disused stretch of line begins on the north side of Fakenham, but the complete infilling of a cutting and the obliteration of any sign of the railway over the first mile northwards by restoration to agriculture make it necessary to begin at the crossing with the B1105. The railway here has become a broad grass track, not dissimilar in character to the nearby Peddars Way (a Roman road) and might, if it were opened to walkers, form a new route for pilgrims to Walsingham, some of whom do still arrive by foot. The track is a farm road and private bridleway, with almost every trace of railway furnishings, including fences, removed.

At the cutting west of East Barsham – and, indeed, east of West Barsham – I was stopped by a gamekeeper who had from a distance mistaken my tripod for a shotgun. He told me that the cutting allowed valuable cover for wildlife, in a region where the farmers have relentlessly cut and burned away anything and everything on the small pieces of land that are not producing crops – and that meant poaching. 'It's going the same way as Lincolnshire, round here, I'm sorry to say,' he told me. 'Nowhere left for the animals to go.' His reaction to my suggestion that the line be made a public path was negative: if that happened, he argued, then the poachers could stroll down here with their dogs and kill hen pheasants on the nest, and no-one would be able to stop them. 'They don't care about breeding. It's a free dinner, isn't it, that's what they say.' As I walked on the hen pheasants did indeed explode from the long grass, and rabbits hopped away in their dozens towards an enormous warren at the northern end.

One small obstacle between here and Walsingham is the removal of a bridge over a farm track, though it is not difficult to get around. North of Walsingham a rubbish tip in a cutting makes a rather more noxious barrier, and the proliferation of cuttings might frustrate some walkers, though there are also embankments giving good views over the open, rolling, very maritime landscape. At Wells the station house still stands, but the yard is in the process of being redeveloped into an industrial estate for light engineering firms. One of the new roads has been renamed 'Great Eastern Way': it points roughly along the route of the line. Just south east of this estate, a number of boats are being kept and repaired along the line. Could there be those at Wells who would like to convert the old railway into a canal? Following the abandonment of the council plan to use the line to make a bypass for Walsingham, there is at least one person who would like to turn it back into a railway: discussions are currently being held.

(Left) Bridge over the lane from West to East Barsham.

(Above) A rare raised view over the East Anglian landscape from a high embankment across the Stiffkey valley. The delectable East Burnham manor house stands in the trees. Rare also are the small fields: this is a surviving pocket of pre-prairie-farming landscape.

(*Above*) *A permanent-way engineer knocks the keys back into place on the line south of Fakenham. The line is used by the magnificent total of one goods train per day, which brings up coal and takes away scrap metal. At one time agricultural produce and paraffin made in Fakenham were*

transported, as well as the products of the now closed and beautiful mill next to the line there. There is talk of complete closure; a society has been formed to do battle.

(*Top*) *A cutting directly north of the Barsham embankment; the cemented brick supports prevent water erosion.*

(*Above*) *North Barsham, from the railway. Only the stile remains to remind that here and there were once separated by a fence.*

(Below) Walsingham. This must surely be the only instance of conversion of a station house into a Russian Orthodox church. Services are held in what was the booking hall: arrival at the right terminus at the other end however is not guaranteed.

(Left) Remains of a signal box, Walsingham.

(Left) Wells-next-the-Sea. The trains came in along the line of the road on the left, by way of a short branch which curved round from the station at the south end of the town.

113

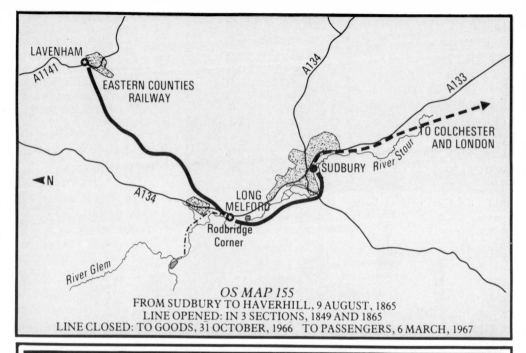

THE COLCHESTER, STOUR VALLEY, SUDBURY AND HALSTEAD RAILWAY

FROM LAVENHAM TO SUDBURY, SUFFOLK (7½ MILES): THE LAVENHAM, MELFORD AND VALLEY WALKS

The C,SV,S&HR was built, in competition with the double-tracked main line route through Bury St. Edmunds and Ipswich, to link Cambridge with Colchester and Clacton, and ran through a series of market and textile towns, of which Sudbury was the most important. Textiles manufactured in the Stour valley included silk, coconut, horsehair and worsted spinning, and all these went by rail. Another line, the Colne Valley and Halstead Railway, ran in parallel to the Stour Valley line down another river valley, leaving it at Haverhill and rejoining it at Chappel and Wake's Colne station. (Halstead is included in the title of the Stour Valley line since the company was originally empowered to build a branch there as well. In the event they did not do so, and another company took over the job.)

The Stour Valley line functioned as a viable alternative to the main line for freight purposes, connected the towns and surrounding villages along it with Cambridge and Colchester and the big wide world beyond, and supplied the east coast resort trade with customers, especially at Clacton. The Bury St. Edmunds to Long Melford branch, originally planned by the Eastern Counties Railway Company, linked the Stour Valley railway with the main line at Bury St. Edmunds and served the agricultural communities between the two, as well as Lavenham which was still a textile town, though it had lost its market 70 years before the railway arrived and already had a shrinking population. After the First World War, all the textile industries in the area went into decline, and the railways declined with them. Since all trains stopped at all stations on the Stour Valley line, passengers travelling long distances would automatically take the much faster Bury–Ipswich–Colchester route, with its streamlined timetabling.

Three short sections of the line between Lavenham and Sudbury are now officially open to the public as paths, largely under the administration of Suffolk County Council. The Lavenham Walk, on the Bury St. Edmunds branch, runs 1½ miles from Lavenham station into a cutting deep between some of the most desolate fields in England, and simply stops dead. You have to go back the way you came, at least as far as the one lane crossing. The cutting sides are very overgrown, though there is a policy of selective clearance which may change this, and its value lies far more in the cover it offers to wildlife than in any aesthetic qualities.

The Melford Walk, also on the Bury branch, is quite likely more useful to its locals since it skirts the back of the village and joins up with a number of tracks and roads there. Between the two the railway has been reclaimed in places, for example directly north of the one-time crossing with the Melford–Lavenham line, which makes walking the route here almost as inadvisable and destructive as trying to walk the average East Anglian footpath – these may be marked on the map as rights of way but more often than not all you find in reality is a signpost pointing vaguely into the middle of a 200-acre field.

One such can in fact be seen at the northern end of the Valley Walk, on the section of the Stour Valley line running between Rodbridge Corner and Sudbury. This is certainly the most useful of the three paths, running parallel with and crossing the Stour, and ending at a poolside picnic area at Rodbridge Corner. The path links with a number of footpaths and bridleways, which would enable walkers to return to the town by different routes, without having to retrace their steps. The stretch nearest to Sudbury station is being made into part of a riverside open space called Friars Meadow, whilst immediately west of this the line passes through Sudbury Meadows, a small stretch of reedy wilderness classified as a Site of Special Scientific Interest.

How very sad, though, that the entire length of line between Sudbury and Lavenham was not acquired for conversion at the times when the railways first closed. I once tried walking between Sudbury and Lavenham: I was on metalled roads for almost the whole distance, and a casual glance at the map of the area will tell you why – there are almost no footpaths. A footpath/cycleway linking with British Rail (and therefore London) at Sudbury, along which people could have gone undisturbed by motors in quest of the Elizabethan past at Lavenham, the best preserved, most dreamlike half-timbered town left in the country (at least, if you go there in Winter or Spring when the coach trade is not operating, and ideally early in the morning): *that* would have been worth having. And the same might be said, with the same force, of the Cambridge line which has been developed for access in two places only; the Clare Castle Country Park, which uses a half mile length at Clare station, and has medieval castle and Victorian station as architectural centrepieces, and two miles of line at Haverhill. Both are useful, but consider how much more useful a long-distance path linking Cambridge and the 'Constable country', which lies some nine miles down-river from Sudbury, would have been. The Suffolk County Council has, however, no plans for extensions of the existing paths.

The most interesting section of the line which I explored is, perhaps predictably, not officially open, and joins the Valley and Melford walks. The complex of Melford station and mill is particularly worth seeing, and only a small area of the large station yard is currently in use, as a coal-haulier's depot. The embankment south of here gives a good view over the flat valley, and is evidently popular with strollers. I met a porky, red-faced Suffolk youth here who had been 'having a few jars' in Melford with his mates and was now following the line to Sudbury where, he said, he knew a pub that stayed open all afternoon and where you could get a pint for 24p. There are pilgrimages and pilgrimages . . .

The still-open Sudbury station is almost as melancholic a place as the ruined station at Glastonbury. It is unmanned; some windows are bricked up, others are boarded over; a bench is padlocked across the stairs to the disused 'down' platform, where one of many chalked-up signs reads

> 'YOU ARE TRESPASS-
> (ING)
> IF YOU ARE ON THIS PLAT
> PICKING BLACKBERRYS.'

The Sudbury 'branch' was formed out of the Stour Valley line by the closure of the line beyond to Shelford and Cambridge, but by ministerial decision the section from Sudbury to Marks Tey was kept open, and since 1974 has been subsidised by central government grant. The line has an extremely energetic and voluble support group in the Sudbury and Marks Tey Rail Users Association (their posters are up on the live platform), who fight to keep the line open, and also – which is the same thing – to encourage the locals to use it. Down the line at Wakes Colne station the Stour Valley Railway Preservation Society (1968) is based: were the branch to close (and it is one of the lines threatened by the British Rail corporate review of August 1979, see p271), they would try to move in themselves, and run their own railway. They also put an intriguing, but now abandoned, proposal entitled 'Walk with Steam' before Suffolk County Council in 1972, for reuse of the Sudbury to Long Melford section as *both* a steam railway and a footpath running side by side. Though inevitably this would mean restrictive and unattractive safety fencing between the two routes, it is nonetheless an idea worth bearing in mind by steam societies who wish to cater for the many visitors who ask to walk up the line to see or photograph the locos as they go by. A similar plan, supported by the Isle of Wight council, using a miniature railway in parallel with a footpath, is currently being put into operation along the west bank of the river Medina. A plan to operate a standard gauge railway in parallel with a footpath between Oakmoor and Alton on the old Churnet valley line in Staffordshire is also to be put into operation, with council blessing.

(Left) Long Melford station. The station house on the left is being kept in a very good state of repair as a private dwelling.

(Top) Signal box at Long Melford. A bridge is out beyond it. Looking north.

(Above) Long Melford: the mill.

(Above) Bridge over the Stour
south of Sudbury, looking
north west.

(Right) Bridge over artificial
inlet to the old mill at Sudbury,
now being converted into a
theatre.

(Top) *Half a mile west of Sudbury station.*

(Left) *Where the rails begin: Sudbury station.*

121

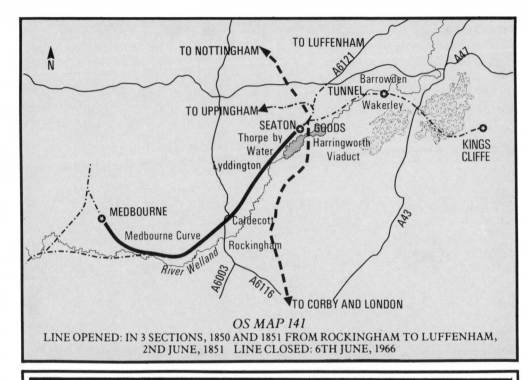

OS MAP 141
LINE OPENED: IN 3 SECTIONS, 1850 AND 1851 FROM ROCKINGHAM TO LUFFENHAM,
2ND JUNE, 1851   LINE CLOSED: 6TH JUNE, 1966

THE RUGBY AND STAMFORD RAILWAY

FROM MEDBOURNE, LEICESTERSHIRE TO KING'S CLIFFE,
NORTHAMPTONSHIRE (16 MILES)

The Rugby and Stamford Railway was begun by the London and Birmingham Railway Company and was later taken over by the London and North Western. It runs up the Avon valley from Rugby and down the Welland valley to join at Luffenham with the Midland Railway's main line between Peterborough and the Derby–Chesterfield industrial complex. In order to streamline its services from Birmingham to Peterborough the L&NW built the line from Seaton to Wansford (opened 1 November, 1879), and thence to Peterborough, knocking 15 miles off the length of its original route along the Midland's line: the new railway became a secondary main line which carried a through service between Birmingham and Harwich until 1939, as well as trains between Birmingham and Yarmouth, and a night mail. The Seaton–Luffenham section dwindled into a single-track branch, whilst another branch from Seaton to Uppingham in Rutland was even less well patronised; here trains were sometimes cancelled for want of a single passenger to use them, though the school supplied a regular number of occasionally destructive customers at certain times of the year. The Medbourne curve was installed in 1883 to link a line operated jointly by the Great Northern and the London and North Western, in order to enable GNR trains to run between Leicester and Peterborough. Until the First World War special trains were operated for the fox-hunting fraternity, whilst the popularity of the hunt in the area was reflected in the renaming of John O' Gaunt station, north of Medbourne, after a local fox covert in the same year that the Medbourne curve was installed, and by the fact that in certain places the railway fences were restricted to 3½ feet in height in order not to impede horses during the chase.

The stretch explored runs through what is for me one of the loveliest but also one of the most frustratingly compromised landscapes in England. From certain angles the broad-bottomed Welland valley with its gently sloping hills looks so 'perfect' that it seems it might have been laid out in reproduction of the work of one of those slightly primitive topographical landscapists of the eighteenth century. From others you can see the chimneys of Corby steelworks, sited just over the hill to the south, and the vast linear molehills made by opencast mining of the local, not very high quality, veins of iron ore – and the illusion of idyll is completely shattered. All in all I think that you can get a better impression of this length of the valley from the lanes that run halfway up the slopes than from the railway, which is sited low and near to the water; but there is at least one section, near Barrowden, where the railway admits you to country unimagined on the roads.

I started my exploration here at Medbourne, attracted by its situation in the centre of a triangle of disused lines (which in the event I did not completely walk). Down by the old station house, now a farm, at the north end of the village I met some boys who had set up their headquarters in a small and solitary railway hut, where they had hung a curtain across the unhinged door and sometimes lit fires in the grate, and fried an egg or two. To them the railway was as much ancient history as the turnpike roads. They did not realise that there had been platforms next to their hut (grassed mounds, looking a little like the surface of a rough hill field, are all that remains) though they told me with great excitement that they knew a lady whose husband – alas, dead – had once been the stationmaster. They had found some old papers in a desk in the hut, and also some old tickets – and lost them again.

Beyond the village the line slopes up steeply and looks as if it might have been farmland for a much longer time than it actually has, an impression that is reinforced in many places later on. For several miles, until you are nearing Seaton, the trackbed is invisible as such, either having been converted back to grassland or to farm roads, though as it is mostly cutting or embankment it retains its engineered shape. The railway seems to have taken pains to harmonise its constructions with the existing architecture here (or was it simply that the stone was cheap then?): a crossing-keeper's house on the lane between Lyddington and Gretton is of Rutland stone, as is the bridge south of Barrowden. In contrast, Leicestershire villages, of which Medbourne is one, tend to be dominated by red brick and the surviving railway constructions here are all of red brick.

Though you can get a good view of the Harringworth viaduct from the old line, it is at present impossible to approach it along the line from the west since Seaton station, which is mostly hidden by a high fence but looks quite well cared-for, is now the site of a scrapyard, and the owners are touchy about letting people through. The viaduct, which was 100 years old in 1978, supports the freight link between Nottingham and London, which goes south via Corby steelworks. I met one of the farmers whose land it crosses. He had been there during the war when the Germans regularly attempted to bomb the viaduct, since it was then of great strategic importance. One would have thought that it was also an easy target, but most of the time the bombers missed; track-laying equipment was kept in the tunnel east of Seaton, and on the few occasions when an arch did get hit it was possible to reconstruct it in a matter of hours. The most dangerous time, the farmer told me, was when the river flooded and the moon was also out, since then the viaduct could be clearly seen from the air, in silhouette against the water.

South of Barrowden the line is particularly pleasant: fine gravel and short grass make for easy walking here, and the embankment gives a good view down into the sheep-pasture and wild small fields that stand on either side of the secretively-winding Welland. After crossing the river you pass the mono-lithic Wakerley limekilns and then climb out of the valley towards King's Cliffe. The bridge crossing over the A43 has been removed and sloped, but is not difficult to negotiate. Another excellent reason for exploring this line is the profusion of fine old villages in the area; in the immediate vicinity of the stretch I walked, Rockingham, Lyddington, Harringworth and Barrowden are all very handsome places, and King's Cliffe (once you get to the original centre) is as attractive an old town at which to alight from a railway journey as you may find.

(Previous page) Medbourne: fine red brick skew arch road-over-rail bridge, now in danger of demolition as 'unsafe'. Looking north west.

(Top left) The line runs parallel with the Welland here, between Medbourne and Drayton.

(Left) Same location: a recurring obstacle for railway walkers – the missing bridge. The bridge here was only for a farm underpass, but the height (20-30') and steepness of the embankment makes progress difficult unless you are determined.

(Above) The embankment south of Seaton gives a good raised railway-traveller's view of the well-known Harringworth Viaduct. It is 1,275 yards long and has 82 arches of 40-foot span.

(Over) South west of Barrowden, looking west: the bridge serves as a farm track.

(Right) Old lime kilns south of the line at Wakerley.

(Below) Brick support construction on the same bridge.

(Bottom) Bridge over the Welland, with Barrowden church.

Great Easton: pedestrian's gate next to level crossing. For reasons I could not imagine, someone had left a pair of knickers on the gatepost.

(Left) High embankment east of the A43. Black poplar is spreading itself across the ash trackbed here, which will soon be as afforested as the land around it.

(Left) King's Cliffe: the very high platform enabled lorries to tip ironstone into waiting wagons.

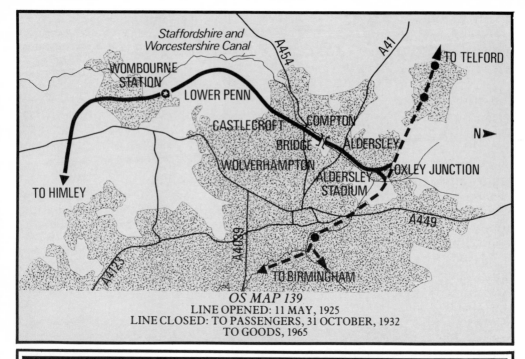

Staffordshire and
Worcestershire Canal

A454

A41

WOMBOURNE
STATION

LOWER PENN

N ▶

TO TELFORD

CASTLECROFT

COMPTON

BRIDGE

ALDERSLEY

WOLVERHAMPTON

ALDERSLEY
STADIUM

OXLEY JUNCTION

TO HIMLEY

A4039

A449

A4123

TO BIRMINGHAM

OS MAP 139
LINE OPENED: 11 MAY, 1925
LINE CLOSED: TO PASSENGERS, 31 OCTOBER, 1932
TO GOODS, 1965

THE KINGSWINFORD BRANCH

FROM OXLEY JUNCTION, WEST MIDLANDS
TO WOMBOURNE, STAFFORDSHIRE (7 MILES)
THE VALLEY PARK AND THE KINGSWINFORD BRANCH RAILWAY WALK

Unusual for its late completion during the grouping years, when many more
lines were being closed than were being opened, the Kingswinford Branch
had had authorisation back in 1905, at a time when Wolverhampton and the
surrounding towns and villages were growing rapidly. The Great Western
delayed construction, however, because of the increase of competition from
bus services. Amongst these was its own bus service from Wolverhampton to
Bridgnorth: the Kingswinford Branch was originally planned as the initial
stage in a rail link between these two towns, but the bus service evidently
proved adequate – at least, the link was never made by rail. A further cause for
delay in completion was the First World War, during which period all work
was halted on the line. When completed the Branch developed into a useful
freight bypass for Wolverhampton, along which traffic travelled between

South Wales and the north of England. It did not prosper as a passenger service, despite the installation of nine halts in twelve miles to make the most of the suburban and ex-urban trade, and passenger trains were quickly withdrawn.

J. Ned Williams' 'By Rail to Wombourn' gives the following details of construction: 'the line . . . seems to have been built by the sweat and toil of large numbers of men and horses, with the only mechanical help from the "steam navvies" and the contractors' light railway. The contractors employed over 200 men. The men worked a 56½ hour week, working six days . . . At one time the work seems to have been sufficiently intense to justify working at night, by the light of oil lamps.' When construction began again in 1919, delays were caused by subsidence, and gangers were advised by Great Western to walk on the sleepers if the ground beneath them suddenly disappeared. One wonders what advice they may have given to drivers in the same situation.

The Kingswinford Branch is a good example of a disused line which runs tangentially to a large metropolitan area; it is also, under the administration of two councils, in the process of being converted to a public path which links the north western suburbs of Wolverhampton with the countryside. The Wolverhampton end is, unfortunately, not at all what it should be: vandalised and strewn with litter, the Aldersley section of the line is very tatty – and, which only makes the criticism more serious, very much in use. Most of the newly-planted trees I saw had failed, and several had been ripped down by those needing to express their hatred for life: there is a policy of replacement, but on the evidence it moves too slowly. A picnic area in which bits of trampled grass were just visible beneath the litter did not invite me to pause and rest, and the grey surfacing material, whilst undoubtedly efficient, only intensifies the waste-ground atmosphere. Further south, despite a lot of dumping and destruction of fencing at entrances, the appearance of the line is a lot less offputting, partly due to a change to a red-coloured surfacing, and to the fact that south of Compton the track runs along a deeply incised cutting (hence the name, Valley Park) which entirely separates the place from the suburbs on either side. Wolverhampton council's system of employing people via the Job Creation Scheme to clean up the path every three to six months is completely inadequate. The result might be that it looks reasonably clean for a day or two, every three to six months, but that is surely not enough.

The Valley Park is in fact not yet complete: a central section north of Compton has yet to be acquired and the park may in time also be extended to incorporate two paths along the Shropshire Union and Staffordshire and

Worcestershire Canals, the latter forming a link with the Staffordshire Way Recreational Path. Fine: but at some point someone is going to have to think long and seriously about how the place appears, and will appear in the future, especially along the Aldersley section where the need for an attractive beginning to this green exit route from the town is the most needed. This statement perhaps requires elaborating: the need is greatest here, first, because this is the point at which the line runs deepest into the urban area and should therefore have qualities which will attract local people on to it, as it were implying the open land which it runs out into by its well-tended greenness in the town itself, and second, because the only effective way to combat the vandalism of council-made amenities is to keep renewing them. If a tireless (and permanently engaged) work force renews trees the day after they have been torn down, and repaints walls the day after they have been scrawled on, then a statement of *care* is made by the authority which employs the work force. And that statement of care, in environmental terms, is exactly what is lacking in so many inner city areas now.

The continuation of the line south from Penn through Wombourne to Himley comes under the administration of South Staffordshire District Council, and it has been christened (in a planning officer's report of October 1978) the Kingswinford Branch Railway Walk. This development is only just beginning, and if the plan is carried through the walk will have features much the same as those of the Wirral Country Park (the Parkgate, Chester and Birkenhead line), with the addition of Trimm tracks for keep-fit enthusiasts and seating, tables and so forth made out of dead trees, old telegraph poles and 'old railway materials'.

The wall may also have a warden. The issue of wardenship is a sticky one: on the one hand, as the Valley Park so clearly demonstrates, the absence of some permanent controlling presence enables all manner of destructive activity to take place: on the other, if the warden or wardens are too prominent in the park or walk, the informal atmosphere is destroyed, and visitors feel (consciously or unconsciously) that they are having an eye kept on them – when the majority are perfectly responsible, and not in any way in need of policing. That wardens of railway walks and similar amenities are generally also cleaners, restorers and ecological managers is clearly a good thing, and may also help to soften the authoritarian outline. At least, one feels, if a warden tells me to pick up my litter from a piece of land that he has just finished planting with wild flowers he will be doing so from the heart, and because if I do not do it, *he* will have to (it is not the responsibility of the police to repair the damage done by criminal action, or to tend the wounds of victims). Nevertheless the image of the 'man in charge' remains, and for this reason the South Staffordshire report's tentative suggestion that the Kingswinford Branch could alternatively be maintained by a group of voluntary 'wardens' drawn from the local community is particularly worth mentioning here. This might well prove a difficult scheme to initiate, but local community care for local community property has been a binding and stabilising influence in our society, and its erosion by the centralisation of effort in local authorities has been one of the key factors in the growth of vandalism in urban areas: such vandalism is enacted by people who do not feel any living relationship with the places in which they dwell. Why not try giving responsibility back to the local people? Why not try to find that tireless work force in the community itself?

(Above & left) Aldersley: line users.

(Above left) Aldersley: where the Valley Park ends and the living railway begins. Beyond the buffer is the Wolverhampton-Telford main line.

(Top right) View from the line, Aldersley.

(Above & right) Urban notice boards. The bridge, over Hordern Road, Aldersley, had been repainted in cream, an ideal base for messages in black felt tip. What answer is there, other than to keep repainting?

(Bottom right) By the Windmill Road entrance, Valley Park.

(Top) Line users, Wombourne. Disused railways provide excellent play areas for children with bikes, with no danger from motor traffic. It should be mandatory that lines in or near urban areas be made accessible to cyclists, especially young cyclists.

(Above) Line users, Wombourne.

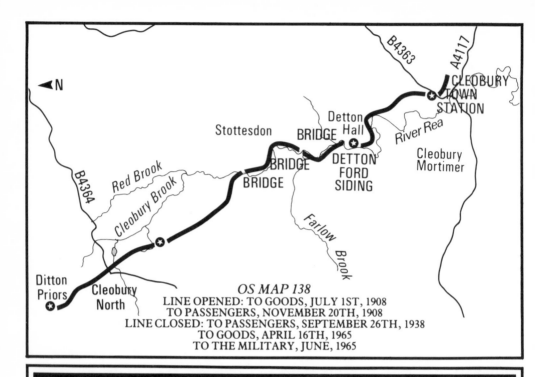

B4363
A4117

CLEOBURY TOWN STATION

Detton Hall

Stottesdon

BRIDGE

River Rea

Cleobury Mortimer

BRIDGE

DETTON FORD SIDING

BRIDGE

B4364

Red Brook

Cleobury Brook

Farlow Brook

Ditton Priors

Cleobury North

OS MAP 138
LINE OPENED: TO GOODS, JULY 1ST, 1908
TO PASSENGERS, NOVEMBER 20TH, 1908
LINE CLOSED: TO PASSENGERS, SEPTEMBER 26TH, 1938
TO GOODS, APRIL 16TH, 1965
TO THE MILITARY, JUNE, 1965

THE CLEOBURY MORTIMER AND DITTON PRIORS LIGHT RAILWAY

FROM CLEOBURY NORTH TO CLEOBURY MORTIMER, (11 MILES).

The CM&DPLR was promoted by two local landowners, Admiral Woodward and Lord Boyne of Burwarton Hall, with the primary intention of exploiting the stone to be quarried from a part of the Brown Clee Hill which lay within Lord Boyne's estate: this 'Dhu' stone was used as railway ballast elsewhere in the network, and in road construction. The line also came to transport stone carried to it from Titterstone Clee Hill by an aerial ropeway which connected with it at a siding at Detton Ford, whilst stone was carried from Brown Clee Hill by means of a 1000-yard long self-acting rope incline similar to the later evolution of the inclines on the Cromford and High Peak Railway. Another earlier and also disused line, the Ludlow and Clee Hill Railway, performed the same kind of function as the CM&DPLR, carrying stone southwards from the Clee Hills to the main line at Ludlow.

The Ditton Priors railway was useful to local farmers, becoming known for its easy-going personal service, dropping off materials next to the line wherever they were needed rather than taking them to the stations where they would have to be picked up and driven back again by road. A passenger service was operated and this was, as might be expected, very slow: it took about 70 minutes to cover the 12½ miles from Cleobury Mortimer to Ditton Priors, partly because mixed trains were run and there were loads to be picked up at the sidings, and partly because of the engineering of the route – there are a number of steep curves, the most severe having a radius of 220 yards, and several gradients of around 1 in 60. Never exactly the biggest railway concern in the country, the CM&DPLR started off with two 0–6–0 locos, named 'Burwarton' and 'Cleobury', and four second hand 4-wheeled coaches off the North London Railway: for reasons uncertain, but probably connected, the line came to be affectionately referred to by Salop enginemen as the 'Piss-Pot and Poker Railway.'

The decline of quarrying – the ropeway closed in 1928, and the Brown Clee Hill quarry operators moved round to the other side of the hill, inaccessible to the railway – might have put paid to the line at an early stage, but a decision by the Admiralty in 1939 to construct an armaments depot at Ditton Priors gave it a new lease of life. As well as the main depot, a huge enclosure swallowing up over a mile of the line – ammunition 'dumps' were also constructed at a number of isolated sidings, and all locomotives on ammunition trains were equipped with 'balloon stack' spark arresters, for obvious reasons. The ammunition trains' speed was sufficiently slow for crew members to be able to shoot rabbits as they were travelling (*shooting* from an ammunition train?), step off to retrieve them and then rejoin the train: the 'blackberry train' of the Craven Arms branch (see next section) may not be wholly fantasy! When the depot closed in June 1965, the railway also closed.

The undulating country to the east of the Clee Hills is complex and steep sided, with a network of lanes that it is not difficult to lose yourself in even with an OS map. But the Ditton Priors branch glides down first a tributary valley then the river valley of the Rea, disguising all complexities in the landscape around it. From the railway the steep hillocks, giving 1 in 7 gradients to some lanes, are little more than gentle rises on one's right or left hand. The line does bend around the valley with noticeable frequency, and there is also a pleasingly frequent alternation of short cuttings with short embankments, and three bridge crossings over the river, all of which are intact. The Rea Valley has been written about at length by a local and at one time popular author called Simon Evans, who was a postman based at

Cleobury Mortimer in the thirties: but he used the roads and footpaths, not the railway, to deliver the mail.

The Royal Navy Ordnance Depot at Ditton Priors is now in use by light engineering and coach building firms, and directly south of this the military fences have been maintained, barring all access. The railway might therefore best be joined at the road crossing east of Cleobury North, though if you were thinking of following the line to the south a detour of a few hundred yards in the other direction would be worthwhile to see the water crane, a rare *in situ* survivor of the original railway furnishings. Travelling south you have a good passenger's eye view of the old buildings of Cleobury North and the hills beyond – a village as it should be, unpolluted with mediocre modern housing designs – and then a gentle right hand bend will lead you on, and on, to the station at Burwarton (this may one day be removed by the Horsehay Steam Trust and reconstructed on their line).

In general then the line is good walking, and would make an excellent candidate for conversion to public access (had it not been sold off to adjacent landowners), passing as it does through entirely unspoiled country, and abutting on Brown Clee Hill at Ditton Priors. And though it may give a simpler picture of the country round it than the lanes do, the line also has its secrets: certain views from certain embankments into corners of the valley which cannot be seen from the roads, certain cuttings where the trees are growing fast, but, as is almost invariably the case, you can see the slightest of depressions in the underbrush where one or two locals pass by at intervals with their guns. This said, I must also mention that south of Prescott a section has already been reclaimed for arable use, and also that not far from there (I am intentionally unspecific) I was stopped by a farmer who utterly forbade me to follow the here intact trackbed across his land. This has been my one experience of the sort. I tried to explain to him that I was working on a book on disused railways, and would have asked his permission if I had known whose permission to ask – over some distance, since he was halfway up the hill and I was in the valley. 'There's no railway there!' he yelled. He was perfectly right about that, of course.

(Right) South of Cleobury North, looking north. A good stretch for dog-roses.

(Above right) Burwarton station.

(Above) In places, nature has 'reclaimed' everything.

(Top) Detail of water crane.

(Right) Water crane, Cleobury North: a device used for letting water into locomotives under gravitational pressure. The guide pipe is of leather. Looking north.

(Previous page) Bridge over the river Rea, west of Stottesdon.

(Top right) Mosses and lichens grow on the trackbed here; it also appears to be in use for grazing. South of the Stottesdon-Norton road.

(Below right) Permanent-way linesman's hut at Detton, once used for shelter and the storage of tools.

(Far right above) Detton: the platform is edged with timber. More grazing here.

(Far right below) Engine shed, Cleobury Mortimer. A cement structure, not likely to be mourned by preservationists. It has recently been struck by lightning.

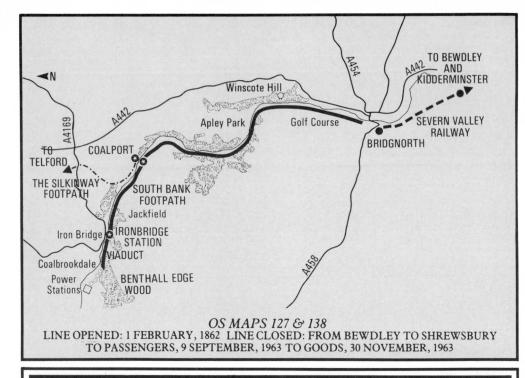

OS MAPS 127 & 138
LINE OPENED: 1 FEBRUARY, 1862 LINE CLOSED: FROM BEWDLEY TO SHREWSBURY
TO PASSENGERS, 9 SEPTEMBER, 1963 TO GOODS, 30 NOVEMBER, 1963

THE SEVERN VALLEY RAILWAY

FROM BRIDGNORTH TO IRONBRIDGE, SALOP (9 MILES): THE SOUTH BANK FOOTPATH AND THE SILKIN WAY

In the early 1850's the still-lingering virus of railway fever hit Bridgnorth. The Severn Railway was then little more than a twinkle fading from the eyes of some (Robert Stephenson himself having been involved in an early, unfulfilled scheme) yet still growing in the eyes of others. *Circa* 1852 the mayor of Bridgnorth is recorded as having said that 'he was sanguine that no more remunerative line would be found in the kingdom' – only given that the new company could also find backers, which until then it had had great difficulty in doing. One of the initiators of the earlier scheme was a man called Robert Roy, who was by all accounts in the railway building business to make a lot of money, and he did indeed eventually make a fortune, though not on the Severn Valley line. His plan, rationally enough, had been to approach the directorate of the Coalbrookdale Iron Company, which was still run by the

Darby family, but he failed to interest the older members of the family in this bright new alternative to the existing system of private lines which ran through Coalbrookdale itself (one of these became a Great Western line, after brief ownership by the Shrewsbury & Birmingham, in 1854).

One of the intentions of the later SVR plan was to provide Shrewsbury with a more direct link with London than it already possessed via Wellington and Wolverhampton. When the line was finally opened in 1862 it connected at Hartlebury with the main London–Birmingham line, run by the Oxford, Worcester and Wolverhampton Railway (known to its users as the 'Old Worse and Worse'). Another link line between Bewdley on the SVR and Kidderminster was completed in 1878, with the intention of streamlining the theoretically profitable connection with the industrial Midlands. The profit in this area remained, however, largely theoretical: more agricultural freight was carried than industrial or manufactured goods, although the railway did serve a coal quarry at Alveley south of Bridgnorth until 1970, seven years after the rest of the line to the north had been closed.

I do not know whether the passenger trains on the SVR were as slow as on certain other country railways, but I was told two anecdotes whilst I was in the area which serve to illustrate the unhurried pace of services on neighbouring lines. The passenger service on the Craven Arms branch, which ran over the Wenlock Edge from a junction with the SVR at Buildwas, was nicknamed 'the blackberry train' by an Edge farmer who used it regularly. This was, he said, because it travelled so slowly that you could get off at the front end, pick a pound of blackberries in one of the cuttings, and hop on again at the rear. Reg Stanley of the Horsehay Steam Trust told me that he once saw a fox escape the following pack, in true story-book fashion, by jumping off a bridge into an open goods wagon as a train trundled by – this was on the Wellington to Market Drayton line, also defunct.

The closure of the whole of the SVR has not been final; as a result of the formation of the new Severn Valley Railway Company (which has already been mentioned on page 46), the line south from Bridgnorth is again operational. It would be pleasant to imagine that the society might, at some point in the future, extend its territory northwards and reanimate the line as far as Ironbridge. It seems especially sad that Ironbridge, 'birthplace of the Industrial Revolution' and since 1968 a museum of industrial archaeology boasting the site of Abraham Darby's blast furnace, the first iron bridge ever built, the Coalport china works and several other unique exhibits, should be without an operating steam railway. But, at least as far as the SVR society is concerned, there is no hope of taking services to Ironbridge: at Bridgnorth itself a bridge has been demolished, a housing estate has just been built across the trackbed, a section has been absorbed into a golf course, and most of the rest has been sold off to farmers and landowners. The very awareness in the planning authorities that helped to create the Ironbridge museum out of a not-so-long-since derelict and decayed town has arrived too late to be of help here: if, with foresight, that bridge had not been demolished, if planning permission to build across the track had been refused . . .

As it is, sections of the line between Bridgnorth make good walking, though the farmers tend to chase walkers off, with some reason here since there is a footpath only yards away, running along most of the right bank of the Severn. West of Apley Park the line has been made into a cinder track, which is a great boon to the valley farms. Before the railway closed access by road here must have been extremely difficult. While it was operating, on the other hand, this secluded stretch of country was linked directly by rail if not by road with the rest of England: 'we were very lucky in that way,' one farmer told me, 'we could get from here to London in less time than you do now, I expect'.

Before Coalport the track has been concreted over for use as a works road, but beyond Coalport as far as Ironbridge power station you can follow it as an official footpath, with adjacent picnic and camp sites. At Jackfield there are some good level crossing gates with ornamental ironwork, whilst in the approach road to the Iron Bridge the rails can still be seen, imbedded in the road surface. The path is for much of its length a gravel track with newly planted trees in some places. It is possible to see the Severn and the steep facing bank along the Jackfield stretch, but west of the Iron Bridge you are in a deep cutting which obscures the view completely, and the path functions primarily as a way of getting into a 'woodland walk', another of the newly organised amenities here. To see the town of Ironbridge itself you must leave the railway and explore: its wonderfully grotesque, steeply-sloping walkways and narrow roads, its slipping, leaning brick houses that seem as if they might have popped up out of the hillside overnight like toadstools, are in the most marked contrast to the straight, flat embankment of the railway.

Running from Coalport into Telford, on the north bank of the Severn, is the Silkin Way: named after the founder of the post-war New Towns, it should be edged in black along its whole length in mourning for the death of what was once a good idea. This is a footpath and cycleway made out of the old London and North Western branch line which connected Coalport and Wellington, closed in 1960. The path was opened in April 1977 but by the time I arrived, 18 months later, the shelters, seats and marker wheels were already badly vandalised, many of the newly planted trees had died without being replaced, and litter had been deposited anywhere except in litter bins. I understand that the policy of management was under review in 1978: just as at Wolverhampton more attention, and no doubt more money, is needed if a path such as this, in close proximity to a vandalism-inducing New Town environment, is to be genuinely pleasant for non-vandals to spend time there.

(Above) Old footpath gate leading to the river Severn, south of Apley Park.

(Top left) Hifnal: dead railway, here in use as a farm road, and dead farm.

(Top right) Coalport station. Mrs Smith occupies the station house with her husband, once a ganger on the line. She worked on the station herself during the war.

(Above) Waiting room on the 'down' platform, Coalport.

(Above) Ironbridge, with the Iron Bridge at left, seen from the site of the station, now a car park. A passenger's eye-view, looking slightly down on the place.

(Left) Buttresses support the site of Ironbridge station. Next to them the old, leaning half-timbered houses with their productive apple trees remain; there before the railway, there after it.

(Above) Viaduct opposite Coalbrookdale, seen from a fisherman's path. Will services ever run over it again?

(Above right) End of the line for walkers: Ironbridge power station. One would have to walk through the middle of the cooling tower to follow the old SVR here. The line does continue beyond the power station, running directly past the ruins of Buildwas Abbey in the direction of Shrewsbury.

(Top left) This marker for the Silkin Way path is a driving wheel off a diesel locomotive.

154

(Left) *The Silkin Way passes underneath . . .*

(Above) *. . . The Hay Inclined Plane, one of the show pieces of the Ironbridge Gorge Museum. The inclined plane, engineered by William Reynolds to begin operation in 1793 and last used in 1894, connects two canals, the Shropshire Canal on the hill, and the Coalport Canal in the valley. The Hay plane was cleared of undergrowth in 1969, and the rails were relaid in 1975, though there is no plan to restore it to working order.*

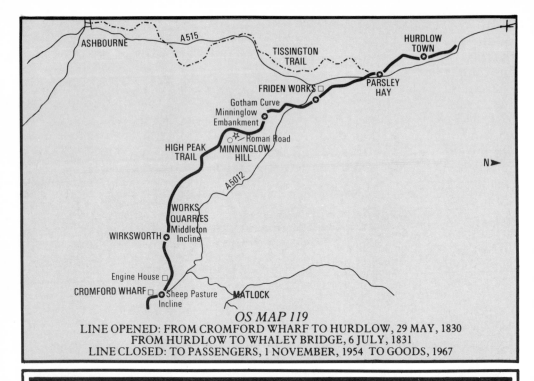

ASHBOURNE · A515 · TISSINGTON TRAIL · HURDLOW TOWN · FRIDEN WORKS · PARSLEY HAY · Gotham Curve · Minninglow Embankment · Roman Road · HIGH PEAK TRAIL · MINNINGLOW HILL · A5012 · N ▶ · WORKS · QUARRIES · Middleton Incline · WIRKSWORTH · Engine House · CROMFORD WHARF · Sheep Pasture Incline · MATLOCK

OS MAP 119
LINE OPENED: FROM CROMFORD WHARF TO HURDLOW, 29 MAY, 1830
FROM HURDLOW TO WHALEY BRIDGE, 6 JULY, 1831
LINE CLOSED: TO PASSENGERS, 1 NOVEMBER, 1954 TO GOODS, 1967

THE CROMFORD AND HIGH PEAK RAILWAY

FROM CROMFORD TO DOWLOW, DERBYSHIRE (17½ MILES):
THE HIGH PEAK TRAIL.

Originally conceived as a tramway, the Cromford and High Peak Railway used stationary steam engines to haul and lower wagons on nine steep inclines. On the level sections horses were used at first, but from the 1840s they were replaced by locomotives. The line was built to link the Cromford Canal and the Peak Forest Canal at Whaley Bridge for the transport of limestone and coal, and was designed by Josiah Jessop, the son of the engineer of the Cromford Canal. Limestone quarries blossomed on either side of the railway, but the founding company was nevertheless in regular financial trouble. A passenger service was operated from 1855 to 1877; the fact that the passengers were required to get out and walk at the inclines, and that the journey along the length of the line took an entire day, may have had a little to do with its early termination. Between 1892 and the First World War the London and

North Western Railway used a section of the line, newly engineered by them for the purpose, to link the then booming spa town of Buxton with Ashbourne, and the main line to London. It was the local passenger service using this route which closed in 1954.

From the engineering point of view the C&HPR is one of the most unusual lines to have been built in England, and retains many relics of its working past, which are now being carefully preserved and in some cases restored to working order. In walking the line I was struck at one and the same time with admiration at the bravado and self-confidence that its founders and engineers must have possessed to initiate the scheme, and with incredulity at the sheer Heath-Robinson battiness of designing a railway, or tramway, or any other kind of a way, that would have to haul up and down nine mountain slopes, the steepest of which has a gradient of 1 in 7. A writer contemporary with the early days of the line reacted in much the same way: he described it as 'the sky scraping High Peak Railway, with its corkscrew curves that seem to have been laid out by a mad Archimedes, endeavouring to square the circle'. ('Strephon', in 'Pictures of the Peak'.)

The C&HPR was converted to a public path and opened as the High Peak Trail by the Peak Park Planning Board in May 1972. It is joined south of Parsley Hay by the Tissington Trail, made out of the line to Ashbourne and opened slightly earlier, in June 1971. As at the Wirral Country Park the trails are used as a central spine which can be walked, or cycled, or ridden on horseback as a thing in itself, or can be used as a means of exploring the countryside around it; side routes are in the process of being signposted. Car parks, picnic sites and toilets have been provided at several old station sites whilst at Hartington on the Tissington Trail a signal box has been restored to working order and is now in use as an information centre. Signposting is generally discreet, in places using indented grey cement markers set at ground level, which fit in well with the 'railway' atmosphere. There has been tree-planting to break up the long thin look and screen windy embankments but in places growth had to be cleared away to keep the track sufficiently wide, and sycamore has been selectively removed as it is an alien species not beneficial to the other flora – a pity, since it is a tree that particularly suits rocky landscapes. The wardens here are called rangers, and one of them is equipped not only with a Land Rover to fulfil his duties, but with a horse. One wonders whether he might not sometimes wear a tin badge and carry a shotgun, or be found at sundown camped underneath one of the railway arches, heating up his beans and coffee.

The work of surfacing the Tissington Trail provides a useful cautionary tale for other developments of the same kind. Most of the High Peak line was ballasted with ash, which was ready made for the easy passage of feet, hooves, or bicycle tyres. The Ashbourne line, however, was laid with limestone ballast and required resurfacing. The Park authority decided to cover the ballast with soil and then seed it, a process which has subsequently been shown to be *more* expensive than the spreading of rolled shale or similar material (as on the Snowdonia Park's path along the Dolgellau Branch), which provides an ideal multi-purpose surface. The Planning Board then found that constant use, especially by horses, was churning up large areas of the turf, which meant that it became necessary to close sections to horse riders and eventually to resurface a 1½ mile stretch between Thorpe and Tissington – with a material similar to rolled shale.

The trails' availability to walkers, horse-riders and cyclists appears to be posing no serious problems by way of conflict between the different modes of travel, and restrictive wooden barriers have not been set up, as at the Wirral Country Park, to keep horses and walkers separate. Since 1975 there has been a cycle hire scheme which enables visitors to ride the trails in either direction and return to their starting point in minibuses which serve walkers in the same way (the bikes go back in a trailer), avoiding the potential tedium of having to retrace steps. On one level this is a good functional scheme which may encourage people to ride bicycles where they would not otherwise do so, and gives beginners a chance to ride out in the country without a single car to make them wobble. But for those with any grain of independence – for those people who fought for the 'Right to Roam' upon which the Peak Park was itself eventually founded, for example; who would anyway be likely, if they were around now, to arrive at the trails using their own bicycles – it must seem a little sad, to say the least, that others are so malleable and unimaginative that they are prepared to ride the officially ratified and approved route like everybody else is doing, and simply leave it at that. In the long run, we really should all be able to find our own way, and extemporise. After all you do not have to be a genius to read an Ordnance Survey map.

It is also well worth noting that the access for cyclists was not planned or desired by the Planning Board, but came about as a result of pressure from the Cyclists' Touring Club. It was only after repeated approaches by the CTC that the original ban on cycling along the Tissington Trail was lifted, at the end of 1972. By September 1976 the Planning Board's official view was diametrically changed: '. . . conversion of the disused railway lines into trails for walking, pony trekking, cycling and nature study has proved a successful project, with every indication of increased annual visitor usage'. (Information document.)

There are two other ex-railways in the area that are open to the public. The first is what was once the Leek and Manifold Valley Light Railway, running between Waterhouses and Hulme End, which closed during the first serious outbreak of railway abandonments in 1934, and was opened as a footpath and bridleway in 1937. The other is the Sett Valley Trail between New Mills and Hayfield, north of Buxton. This is three miles long and was opened in the summer of 1976. Another very promising project for conversion currently being negotiated by the Park Planning Board is the line from Rowsley to Peak Forest, which closed in 1968. The Peak Railway Society applied to reopen the line between Buxton and Matlock using a steam and diesel service, but were given permission to operate only on the short section between Buxton and Peak Forest Junction. When this railway first opened, Ruskin wrote in his 'Praeterita' –

'There was a rocky valley between Buxton and Bakewell . . . divine as the vale of Tempe; you might have seen the gods there morning and evening, . . . You enterprised a railroad, . . . you blasted its rocks away . . . And now, every fool in Buxton can be at Bakewell in half-an-hour, and every fool in Bakewell at Buxton.'

Officially speaking, no fool may pass that way at present, until the plan is settled. But it is good to think that in this case the walkers' lobby has the upper hand and that the railroad may in time become a path whereby solitary romantics can enter the once again divine valley, and contemplate its resettled gods.

(Above left) Cromford Wharf, on the Cromford Canal. The chimney belongs to Leawood Pump House (1849), used to raise water from the Derwent to maintain the canal's water level: it is currently being restored to full working order. Loads were transferred at the wharf from barge to railway wagon and vice versa. The building now functions as a field centre. The canal is also being restored, and it is possible to walk both ways from here along the towpath. Looking west.

(Left) Hawser return pulley, at the bottom of Sheep Pasture Incline; this was installed only a few years before the railway closed. Nearby are a water tank used both by the locomotives and the stationary steam engine, and a workshop where the haulage chains and locomotives were maintained. The latter is being converted into an information centre. A few hundred yards up the incline is a pit designed to catch runaway wagons. It worked – one is buried in the mud there.

(Above) Ganger's hut, halfway up the incline. The combination of leaf-fall and stone gives a landscaped garden look. The three persons in the window had been admiring a nearby graffito carved into the rock in Roman letters and dated August 13, 1891. In the old days they took real trouble, and their work will be remembered.

161

(Above) Sheerleys tripod crane, with main pulley wheel missing, in a quarry at the side of the Sheep Pasture Incline.

(Right) Sheep Pasture Incline: man-made rock face, and rock flora.

(Far right) View from near the Sheep Pasture engine house. Between here and Middleton Top the line passes through a landscape of quarries and ex-quarries, sometimes capped by overhanging woods, which can be as striking as the natural formations and look for all the world like details out of paintings by Elsheimer.

(Left) Minninglow Embankment. Too-frequent comparisons with ancient history may be invidious, but I defy anyone to stand in front of this massive stone construction without being reminded of medieval castle architecture. It is 300 yards long, and was buttressed around 1900. Minninglow Tumuli stand one mile back along the line, on its northern side, but at present there is no right of way to them: there should be. Looking north west.

(Above) Farm underpass, Minninglow Embankment. A mile further up the line you come to the aptly-named Gotham Curve, one of the tightest bends on any railway in the country, which turns through an angle of 80 degrees and has a radius of 55 yards. Short wheel-based engines were used and the maximum speed was 5 m.p.h.

(Right) Middleton Top Engine House contains a 20 h.p. condensing beam engine constructed in 1829, the only survivor of eight similar apparatuses in use when the railway was first opened. Water for the boilers was kept in reservoirs nearby. The engine is restored and will eventually be worked for visitors.

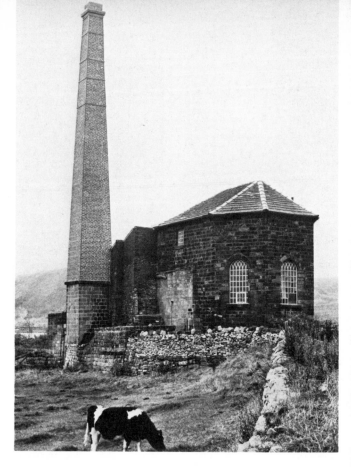

(Right) Hauling wire at the top of Middleton Incline, which has a gradient of 1 in 8½. Initially there was one track, but in 1894 it was doubled and ran in this form till 1963. The double track made it possible to dispense with the beam engine and offset one loaded and three empty wagons ascending against two loaded or five empty wagons descending. Looking west.

(Above) Newhaven tunnel,
under the A515, looking south
west. The 'Cromford and High
Peak Railway Co.' insignia
can be found here, on the
western end.

(Left) Junction of High Peak
(on the left) and Tissington
Trails; south of Parsley Hay,
looking south.

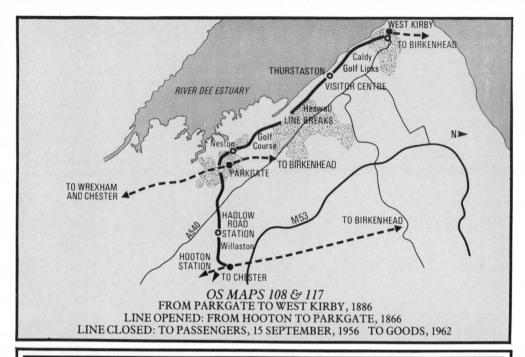

OS MAPS 108 & 117
FROM PARKGATE TO WEST KIRBY, 1886
LINE OPENED: FROM HOOTON TO PARKGATE, 1866
LINE CLOSED: TO PASSENGERS, 15 SEPTEMBER, 1956 TO GOODS, 1962

THE PARKGATE, CHESTER AND BIRKENHEAD JUNCTION RAILWAY

FROM WEST KIRBY TO HOOTON, MERSEYSIDE (12 MILES):
THE WIRRAL COUNTRY PARK

There is evidence that the original plan for this railway was that it should be extended from Parkgate across the Dee estuary to Flint on the Welsh shore, in the process reclaiming 8,000 acres of land from the sea. Nothing came of this – though a ferry service from Parkgate probably operated instead – and twenty years after the first section was completed the line was run alongside the estuary instead of across it, with the intention of forming a link with the Wirral Railway at West Kirby. This link was not achieved end to end, and passengers travelling both lines would not only have to change trains but stations as well.

The primary purpose of the P,C&BJR was to serve a colliery at Neston: the line carried produce and supplies for Wirral farmers, and before the silting of the Dee estuary finished Parkgate's operations as a port, fish was also transported. What was almost certainly not anticipated by the founding company was that the railway would become an important commuter link, carrying workers out of the Merseyside urban centres into a rapidly proliferating suburban sprawl under which a large part of the Wirral peninsula gradually disappeared, and which the railways were directly responsible for creating. There were enough 'better class' commuters for a peak period service from Heswall to have had a club carriage, fitted with armchair seats and bridge tables, up to the beginning of the First World War. At this time too the railway did good business at weekends, carrying day trippers out of Liverpool and Chester to Parkgate and West Kirby, which were then popular as seaside (or in Parkgate's case, marshside) resorts. The track was a single line with passing places, and there were turntables at West Kirby and Hooton, though these were rarely used. The now cherishingly preserved station at Hadlow Road, Willaston is typical of those erected by the London and North Western during the later period when it and the Great Western ran the line jointly.

Cheshire County Council was one of the first local authorities to make practical recognition of the possibilities of disused railways as recreational facilities, though it is worth noting that they had first to be prompted by a group of voluntary organisations based in the Wirral, who had drawn up a scheme for a 'Wirral Way' – the phrase is now used to describe the railway line part of the country park – which would have used the line and then continued to Chester via a footpath and canal towpath. (This was at a time when the Wirral peninsula was still a part of Cheshire and 'Merseyside' did not exist as an administrative region.) As a result of this stimulus, Cheshire County Council's paper 'Cheshire Countryside, a Scheme for a Wirral Country Park' was published in 1968, and the Wirral Country Park became one of the first two country parks recognised and funded by the Countryside Commission under the 1968 Countryside Act.

Two major justifications for the park, which opened in 1973 and by July 1977 had cost £350,000 to develop and has a yearly running budget of about £97,000, were the pressure of population on the remaining Wirral countryside, and the congestion of roads linking Liverpool and the Wirral with North Wales. The idea – and it is the same principle that all subsequent country parks have been based upon – was to divert or entice the frustrated occupants of ten-mile-long traffic jams along roads to distant beauty spots into somewhere that was local, easy to drive to, and where large numbers of people could be managed with relative ease. The management here is again carried out by rangers, symbolically uniformed in green: these comprise a head ranger, a senior ranger, four ordinary rangers, and part-timers for peak periods. The park also has cleaners, information personnel, and a warden for its camp site. The diversion of local people has clearly been effective: in 1977 it was estimated that the park was receiving around half a million visitors per annum on its 200 acres of ground.

One of the main difficulties encountered in setting up the Wirral Country Park was the opposition of local landowners, or people (and there are many of them) whose houses backed on to the old line. This is likely to be so wherever development for public access takes place. To quote from an official information sheet: 'many locals took a great deal of convincing that what we were doing was sensible. There was a great fear of the unknown.' Nonetheless the locals were convinced, and the park is sufficiently respect-worthy now for it to be able, for example, to negotiate with owners of adjacent land in order to enable the public to use private lanes or paths, thus improving access even further.

The Wirral Way includes ten miles of bridleway especially created by splitting the line along its middle, and either keeping one of the streams of traffic on an embankment or making a fence division. Arguably necessary in such a high-pressure area as this, these fences are at present severe in their effect, and function as a visual statement of authoritarian control over the 'informal' environment. I understand that they are being screened with hedges, which may help to soften this impression. The park has also succeeded in annexing another 15 miles of footpaths and bridleways to itself – these it calls 'sidetracks' – as well as areas of land (one, at Thurstaston, where a visitor centre is now nicely sited, was a Second World War anti-aircraft gun emplacement) next to the still-lovely Dee foreshore. From this point of view the Wirral Country Park is particularly noteworthy: it is not always enough to convert disused railways into paths or bridleways – they may be simply boring unless visitors are given a chance to get *off* them, and find other angles on the country they are in. There are also facilities for barbecueing and fishing here, and a strong emphasis is placed upon education: the park is managed where possible as a nature reserve and the consciousness-level of the casual visitor is raised by such things as the establishment of signposted nature trails, controls over the picking of wild flowers, reserved areas for wildlife conservation, labelled geological exhibits, and a repeated emphasis on the flora and fauna of the park in the several leaflets available, which include a monthly newsletter full of vigorously enthusiastic writing on the beauties of nature to be seen in the park. A slide programme is run at the Visitor Centre, guided walks are operated from July to September, and a 'teacher's pack' can be obtained giving detailed information on local history, geology, natural history, climate, as well as a short account of when the park was once a railway.

There has been a certain amount of successful tree planting, using trees and shrubs indigenous to the locality, and boundary hedges have been replaced, especially when screens for housing development are required. Erosion of grassland and other plantlife is inevitable given the numbers who use the park, and this is monitored: new paths are not always fenced off and re-seeded – if they seem to be useful then the rangers may decide to build them in by improving the surface or putting in steps. Since the park has been established vandalism has not been a major problem (contrast the Valley Park, or the Teesside paths): the explanation for this, of course, is the sustained presence of the rangers. There is very little litter, which is cleaned up when it is found, and when they can the rangers will get litter-bugs to pick up their droppings – another aspect of the education process?

All this amounts to a carefully planned and highly organised set of recreational facilities, which is undoubtedly a model for other projects of the same sort. My criticism of the result as an *experience* is that whilst I can see that there is good reason for the linear fences, the barriers at entrances to prevent motorcycles getting in, the signs (in places, for example at Thurstaston, as with certain road junctions, you are looking at a landscape of signs pointing, or signs labelling), and the rangers themselves directing the traffic in the car parks and generally keeping an eye on things, the result is that it is difficult to forget that you are in an Official Place. The informal has been formalised. Given the circumstances, it is at least understandable how this has come about, but guiding and restriction, however necessary or well intended they may be, always act towards an erosion of the independence and spontaneity of those being guided. The 'escape' from the nearby urban areas is, therefore, highly qualified, and no real substitute for an energetic hike along the Clwydian mountains, even if the latter can only be attained at weekends by risking a wait in a ten-mile-long traffic jam.

THURSTASTON 2¼.
HOOTON 12.

(Above) West Kirby: the starting point at the northern end. Once more, the backs of other people's houses.

(Left) West Kirby. An old-style park with lakes and rosebeds, etc, is beyond the trees on the right; the horse ride begins beyond the bridge.

173

(Above) Caldy: pedestrians on the left, equestrians on the right. But what about the cyclists?

(Right) Thurstaston. A motorist enters the car park; a bicycle is parked where the locos once ran. In the background are new buildings constructed to accommodate staff, and 'intended to invoke the character of a rural estate community'.

174

(Above) View over the Dee estuary, from the embankment south of Gayton.

(Left) Gayton: remains of a rail-over-road bridge adjoining the golf course.

175

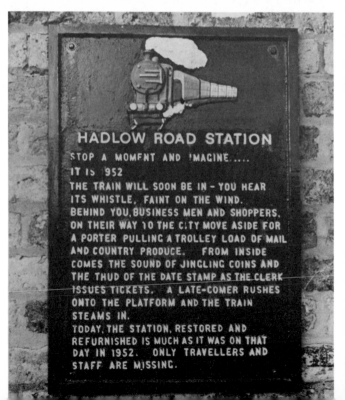

HADLOW ROAD STATION
STOP A MOMENT AND IMAGINE.....
IT IS 1952
THE TRAIN WILL SOON BE IN – YOU HEAR
ITS WHISTLE, FAINT ON THE WIND.
BEHIND YOU, BUSINESS MEN AND SHOPPERS,
ON THEIR WAY TO THE CITY MOVE ASIDE FOR
A PORTER PULLING A TROLLEY LOAD OF MAIL
AND COUNTRY PRODUCE.   FROM INSIDE
COMES THE SOUND OF JINGLING COINS AND
THE THUD OF THE DATE STAMP AS THE CLERK
ISSUES TICKETS.   A LATE-COMER RUSHES
ONTO THE PLATFORM AND THE TRAIN
STEAMS IN.
TODAY, THE STATION, RESTORED AND
REFURNISHED IS MUCH AS IT WAS ON THAT
DAY IN 1952.   ONLY TRAVELLERS AND
STAFF ARE MISSING.

(Right) Memory line . . . At
the bookstall at Thurstaston
idyllic watercolours of the
railway are on sale.

(Above) Hadlow Road
station, Willaston. Here you
can play at being a train on a
genuine track with no fear of
getting squashed.

(Left) End of the country park
at Hooton. Beyond the fence is
the Birkenhead to Chester line.

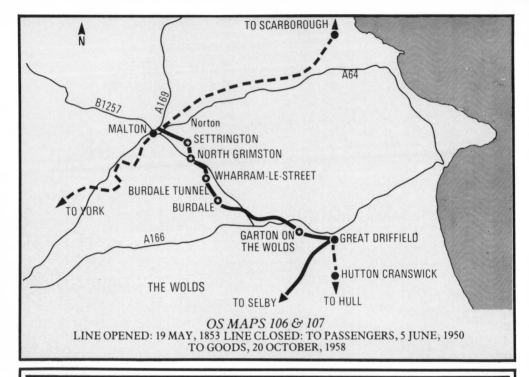

OS MAPS 106 & 107
LINE OPENED: 19 MAY, 1853 LINE CLOSED: TO PASSENGERS, 5 JUNE, 1950
TO GOODS, 20 OCTOBER, 1958

THE MALTON AND DRIFFIELD RAILWAY

FROM NORTON, NORTH YORKSHIRE TO GREAT DRIFFIELD, HUMBERSIDE (20 MILES)

The Malton and Driffield Railway was an independently built line crossing the Yorkshire Wolds, and had gradients of between 1 in 104 and 1 in 64: another branch from Driffield to Frodingham Bridge was projected by the same company but never begun. The line was opened on the same day as another line from Malton to Pilmoor. It is a good example of a service which may not have ever had a high passenger usage, but nonetheless provided an invaluable service to the rural communities and farms of its area, especially in winter. Even after it had been officially closed to passenger traffic, the railway continued to fulfil this fundamental role in difficult weather for so long as it was used as a goods route, giving lifts to people who would otherwise have been irretrievably stuck on the hills. After the railway closed for good there were, and will continue to be, times when these communities are once more entirely cut off by snowdrifts which make the roads useless for 'alternative' vehicular transport.

At Malton I was lucky enough to meet Ron Benson, who started on the railways in 1943, knew the line between Malton and Driffield well having worked it as a driver, and is still working. The Burdale tunnel was one of the first subjects which came up, and the strongest image in Ron Benson's mind was of the icicles which formed on the tunnel roof in winter, and of the spray of icy water which driver and fireman would have to endure at such times. One of the guards, Bill Blades, who when he retired asked to ride up in the cab on his last run, no doubt remembers that spray quite as well if not better. No-one warned him about the wet, which in his many passages through the tunnel he had never imagined, sitting in his guard's van. As they approached the driver and fireman sneaked on their waterproofs whilst Bill Blades rode on, in his innocence, dressed only in a guard's uniform . . .

The Burdale tunnel was also clear in the memory of two other railwaymen I chatted with: the station master at Driffield, who had been a ganger on the line, said it was 'murder' working in the tunnel, and that 'everything there was covered with black slime' whilst Jim Appleby, another one-time ganger, told me 'it had a smell all its own' and vividly described the experience of ducking back into one of the refuges when a whistle-blast warned that a train. was approaching. Jim Appleby, incidentally, lives in a house next to the operational Driffield–Bridlington line. It is a quiet house, in quiet country. As we were talking a high speed train went past, filling the room with about as much noise as a single articulated lorry, and was almost instantly inaudible again. Idly I wondered, how many articulated lorries would have had to roar past in order to get the same load as that train was carrying to its destination?

Ron Benson was able to tell me how the line had served the quarries at Burdale and Wharram le Street. These were the line's main justification in fiscal terms, and supplied 99% pure chalk to the steel mills at Redcar. The chalk went out from Burdale in train loads of nine waggons as far as Wharram, where the load was doubled to eighteen. The amounts carried were massive, as anyone who stands in the Burdale quarry will have not much difficulty in guessing: as an example, K. Hoole records ('Regional History', IV) that in 1925, 104,808 tons of chalk were removed in 7885 wagons. In the Second World War the line had strategic importance as a carrier of armaments to an emplacement at Southburn, between Driffield and Pocklington, whilst in day-to-day affairs it operated a goods service to the local farms, carrying milk daily to the dairy at Driffield. Passengers included the pupils of Bridlington High School, and at weekends visitors to Driffield and Malton markets, and day-trippers to Bridlington's sea front. There were also specially decorated excursion trains put on for Hull fair: one of these was pulled by loco 381 which had a cannon bullet imbedded in it, a souvenir from an air attack on Pickering engine shed. There were, however, no Sunday trains as a result of an agreement with a local landowner, so that excursion trains had to be re-routed via Scarborough.

Then there were the disasters, and this stretch seems to have had its share. At Settrington in 1950, loco 5648 derailed and sailed into somebody's living room, though luckily no-one was in at the time; at Burdale Harold Preston was driving when the train came out of the tunnel and killed a baby on the line; and at Garton 'slack', also with the unlucky Harold Preston driving, a locomotive ploughed into a lorry on a farm crossing during the Second World War and killed seven Italian prisoners of war – as a result of this a cutting side was removed and a whistle board was erected where it had clearly been needed long before. Ron Benson also told me of how his father, a driver before him, had started getting ulcers after his locomotive went over a man on the line at Sledmere: when he stopped, he found the victim's head seated grotesquely on top of a big end. Ron Benson himself says he has a fear of automatic level-crossing barriers: somehow he cannot be *absolutely* sure that they will always do their job and stop the traffic before he gets there. 'Of course,' he summed up philosophically, 'there are stories like that on any line.'

One last detail, from the station master at Driffield. He had been one of those involved in the immense labour of relaying the tracks along the Malton and Driffield line. But it had turned out to be labour in vain, since the line was closed a few months after the work was completed! They then had to take the tracks up again. This does leave the possibility, I suppose, that British Rail might one day reopen the line for use out of sheer administrative absent-mindedness.

(Right) Live and dead . . .
The old track continues north
west over the York-
Scarborough main line, to
connect with the York-
Darlington line south of
Thirsk.

(*Above*) *Norton industrial estate. The line ran to the right of the fence, through what is now the property of Porkshire Ltd. The air here is heavy with the smell of bacon being smoked, and seagulls circle overhead. During the flood of 1947 all the locos in Malton and Norton were moved up here, where there were then four sidings.*

(*Left*) *View from the embankment.*

(*Over*) *West of Wharram le Street the ash embankment, now a farm road, leads up into a Wolds valley.*

(Top) Wharram: the left branch leads into what was the chalk quarry, with the stone-crusher still standing. The quarry is now a nature reserve under the protection of the Yorkshire Naturalists' Trust.

(Above) Ganger's hut. Before this cutting it is possible to alight from the deserted Victorian railway at the deserted Medieval village site of Wharram Percy which was abandoned, probably, at the beginning of the sixteenth century.

(Top left) Burdale quarry, also now disused.

(Centre left) Burdale station. The line winds down the valley from here on a low but clearly-defined embankment.

(Lower left) Burdale station: supports for a coal depot siding in the foreground.

(Above) North of Wetwang. Much of the line here has been reclaimed or converted to farm roads that bear no trace of ever having been a railway. At Driffield the track connects first with another disused line running from Selby through Market Weighton, then with the operational Hull-Bridlington line.

185

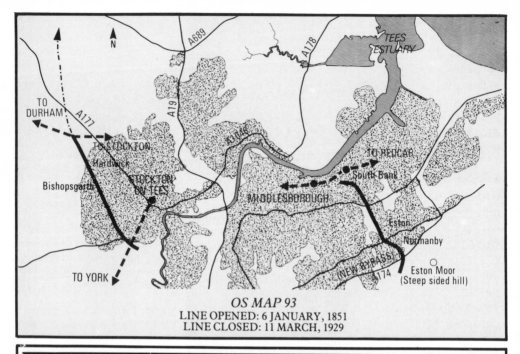

OS MAP 93
LINE OPENED: 6 JANUARY, 1851
LINE CLOSED: 11 MARCH, 1929

THE ESTON BRANCH AND THE CASTLE EDEN BRANCH

THE ESTON BRANCH
FROM SOUTH BANK TO NORMANBY, CLEVELAND (2½ MILES)

It is a part of the urban development policy for Teesside that a system of walkways be created, to which local paths will eventually be linked. A central path already runs along the Tees from Middlesbrough Dock out into the country area near the confluence of the river Leven. It sounds like a promising plan. I decided to explore two stretches of redeveloped line to find out what it had so far produced, in practice, from the area's old railways.

This short branch was opened to serve a mine at Eston, south of Normanby, where the main seam of Cleveland ironstone had been discovered in 1850: W. W. Tomlinson describes this discovery as 'an event of incalculable importance, commercially, to the North of England' ('The North Eastern Railway', p. 507). The branch connected with the Middlesbrough and Redcar Railway, and along it went vast quantities of ironstone to blast furnaces built by Messrs. Bolcklow and Vaughan at Witton Park in 1846. The branch itself was constructed by Bolcklow and Vaughan, but the Middlesbrough and Redcar Railway belonged to the Stockton and Darlington Company, and the new traffic helped to get the railway company out of the serious financial difficulties which it was in at the time. Subsequently the line was also used for passenger traffic: in 1854 a return ticket from Eston (which had by then grown into quite a large mining community) to Middlesbrough on a Saturday evening market train was 3d.

The Eston Branch provides the more useful 'green' outlet of the two lines, at least potentially, for a central urban area. It starts two miles east of Middlesbrough town centre, running out from the worm-eaten heart of a very decayed urban area of rowhouses and demolition sites known as South Bank towards the North York Moors. The National Park boundary is, in fact, only three miles south of the conurbation, and the Eston branch runs towards it with the landmark of Rosebery Topping beyond its southernmost end. Given just a little imagination, and just a little money, (deflected perhaps from the massive scheme to circle the entire urban area with road bypasses), this old railway could act as a connector between the urban wasteland of South Bank and the very beautiful, life-regenerating moorland hills.

As it is, you can indeed walk or cycle the path but who – at least at the northern end – would want to do so? Other than the insertion of a kink or two in the tarmac laid at some points, about as much thought and care has gone into this very ungreen 'greenway' as goes into a supermarket car park. The route needs many, many trees (I understand that some have been planted, but at least at the northern end I was not aware of more than a handful); it needs thick, high hedging; it needs ample screening for industrial buildings; it needs flowers, in a place where there are no flowers! And before any of this, it needs keeping clean; when I was there, there was litter under every surviving bush.

The path looks a lot better at the Normanby end, where it has been well fenced off from surrounding houses and trees have been planted, and survive. But Normanby is a better-preserved, more affluent part of the conurbation: this looks very much like a case of 'unto every one that hath shall be given'. Finally, the path does not make the link with the moors that it could do. It ends officially (and for cyclists, effectively) at the housing estate illustrated, continuing south of the ring road as a very muddy, narrow track obviously much in use despite its lack of recognition. It could readily be connected with the paths leading up the steep scarp slope of Eston Moor.

(*Left*) *North of the A175 the line still operates, though infrequently, to serve a scrapyard and riverside industry. The local children seem to enjoy this stretch better than the official footpath.*

(*Above*) *The horse is tethered to a post holding a newly-planted tree: there are stables nearby, whilst immediately north of this a wide 'green' made out of waste land is grazed by other horses, some of which belong to gypsies.*

(Above) Generation beyond generation: heavy competition for space on this sad notice board (a wall of a road-over-rail bridge) has led to the use of bigger and thicker lettering, 'DOBO and BAZIL' are already nearly invisible: 'BOOT BOYS' are on their way out.

(Right) Distant goal beyond the last housing estate: the North York Moors. The line, which branched here, has been obliterated by the foreground landscaping, but continues through the bushes at the right.

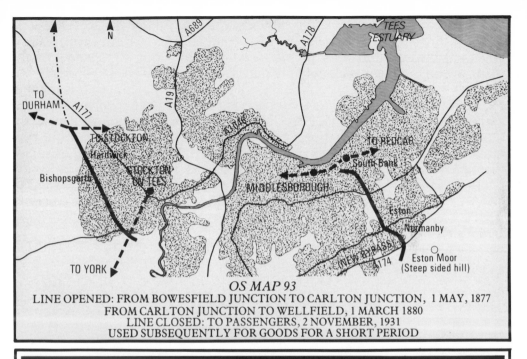

OS MAP 93
LINE OPENED: FROM BOWESFIELD JUNCTION TO CARLTON JUNCTION, 1 MAY, 1877
FROM CARLTON JUNCTION TO WELLFIELD, 1 MARCH 1880
LINE CLOSED: TO PASSENGERS, 2 NOVEMBER, 1931
USED SUBSEQUENTLY FOR GOODS FOR A SHORT PERIOD

THE ESTON BRANCH AND THE CASTLE EDEN BRANCH

THE CASTLE EDEN BRANCH
FROM HARDWICK TO HARTBURN, CLEVELAND (3¼ MILES)

This line was created by the North Eastern Railway Company in order to make a connection between Stockton and the West Hartlepool to Sunderland line west of Castle Eden, and it forged a rail route through an agricultural area more than amply surrounded, but not itself served, by railways. The first section opened, between Bowesfield Junction at Thornaby (South Stockton) and Carlton Junction (later renamed Redmarshall Junction), was from 1915 a part of an electrified mineral route. There was never a regular passenger service on this section, though there was one on the remainder of the branch. As the line made a direct link between Leeds and Sunderland, it was planned at the beginning of the century to convert it into a secondary main line, and a curve was installed in 1901 which diverted traffic off the Leeds Northern line from Egglescliffe to Stockton. But the Corporation of Stockton, presumably

191

fearing that the effect of traffic missing the town might be to cause it to dwindle into a post-industrial nonentity, complained to the railway company, and the railway company – for whatever reasons – quickly abandoned the plan: the link curve was closed only one year after it had been opened.

Work is still in progress on the redevelopment of the line, so it is perhaps too early to make any constructive observations. The work involves regrading and drainage of the earth trackbed, but I did not see any attempts to make the line into a genuinely attractive route. Like the Kingswinford Branch it runs tangentially to the conurbation rather than into it, but it does nonetheless pass through a series of dreary modern housing estates, with more in the process of being erected. Their occupants might well be grateful for a tree-shaded, clean, grassed exit to their estate world, leading out towards County Durham. As it is . . .

(Far left) The branch is bisected by the Durham main line, but this has not prevented the formation of paths down and up the embankments. Here however, supply will eventually rise to meet demand: the County Council is developing the branch as a path as far north as the county boundary (another four miles), though in the process they propose to demolish two viaducts – and also, you may note, to construct a footbridge here. Looking north.

(Top left) Line users, just before the urban boundary at Hardwick. They did not know their playground had been a railway.

(Centre left) Hardwick: a very uninspiring route through a very uninspiring housing estate. But think what tall trees could do here.

(Lower left) Bishopsgarth: view from road-over-rail bridge.

193

(Above) Hartburn: passenger's-eye-view of semi-detached suburbia.

(Top) Hartburn: typical sloping of embankments following bridge removal. A steep, unattractive cinder path has been made on the near side.

(Right) The back end of town, Hartburn. The land here is criss-crossed with spontaneous paths made by fishermen and children, and the railway is now just one of these. The removal of a bridge over the York-Stockton line, beyond this, truncates the route.

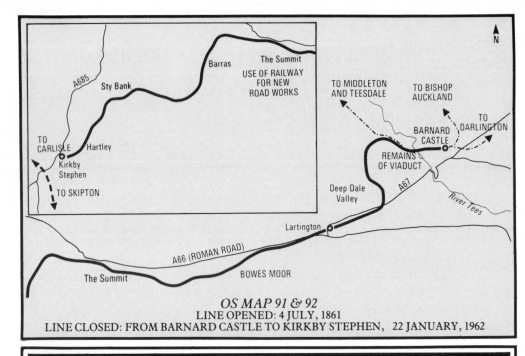

OS MAP 91 & 92
LINE OPENED: 4 JULY, 1861
LINE CLOSED: FROM BARNARD CASTLE TO KIRKBY STEPHEN, 22 JANUARY, 1962

THE SOUTH DURHAM AND LANCASHIRE UNION RAILWAY

FROM BARNARD CASTLE, COUNTY DURHAM TO KIRKBY STEPHEN, CUMBRIA (23 MILES)

The SD&LUR was a subsidiary of the Stockton and Darlington Company, and started this trans-pennine line from Tebay (west of Kirkby Stephen) to Barnard Castle with the sole purpose of transporting iron ore from Lancashire to the blast furnaces at Teesside, and transporting coal and coke in the reverse direction. Navvies constructing the line received 3s. 1d. to 3s. 4d. per day, and masons 5s. a day, whilst the constable hired to keep an eye on the navvies and prevent them poaching on the moors as they built the line across it, received £1 1s. per week, plus 1s. 6d. per month 'boot allowance': presumably he got through quite a few inches of boot leather in the execution of his duties. Once opened, the line functioned as planned but was blocked many times by snowdrifts at the highest point, sometimes for weeks. Single track was used in the original construction but was doubled in three stages in 1867, 1873 and

1874, which necessitated the rebuilding of three of the viaducts. The eastern section of the line between Barnard Castle and Spring Gardens Junction was opened on 1 August, 1863, and enabled traffic to move directly between Bishop Auckland and the west.

I chose to walk the section between Barnard Castle and Kirkby Stephen because it gives a directly east–west route across the Pennine range, and a very rewarding exploration this turned out to be. In the first place both Barnard Castle and Kirkby Stephen are delightful small towns, Barnard Castle being the more impressive of the two, poised next to its medieval castle above the Tees, and make excellent beginning and finishing places for a rail-less railway journey. In the second place the country is superb, especially when you reach the high point above the Vale of Appleby from which the line winds intricately down and around the contours, giving fine views at almost every point.

At Barnard Castle the station site is completely gone. Disoriented by the new building there I asked a local, who explained that the line had run through what is now the reception of Glaxo laboratories, and that the station had stood where there is now a tennis court. Furthermore, if you were to try to follow the line directly west from here you would in a very short time plunge several hundred feet to a horrible death on the rocky shore of the Tees, since the viaduct which once spanned the gorge there has been demolished. Acts of vandalism are not perpetrated solely via the crowbar and the spray can; it is also perfectly possible to vandalise things of nobility and beauty via the blandly civilised mechanisms of committee decision. The difference alas, is that committees do not get arrested. The Tees viaduct had in fact been engineered by Thomas Bouch, made eternally notorious by the collapse of his bridge over the river Tay, but unlike the Tay bridge this viaduct did not collapse during use, and would not have collapsed if some responsible body had found the funds to maintain it. In the event, British Rail consulted Durham County Council, who made no objection to demolition since they had no plan to convert the line to a path of any sort (they should have had); no-one, apparently, raised an organised protesting voice, and this magnificent structure and *enhancement* of the river landscape was pulled down in the mid-70's. Nor was it the only viaduct to go along this line: the Belah and Deepdale viaducts, metal structures also by Bouch, with pylon-like supports which had the delicate and decorative appearance of lace from certain angles, were demolished at the same time. (To set the record straight, however, I should mention that Durham County Council have taken a good many other viaducts under their wing, on lines now open or about to be opened as paths.) Even so, the viaducts of the SD&LUR should have been preserved – if not by the council, then by British Rail itself, until some other proprietor could be found.

The two end-pieces of the Tees gorge viaduct remain, still impressive, built of the local stone which is gold until it has weathered, when it turns to greenish-grey, like the colour of the surrounding tree trunks. The horrible fall I mentioned is in fact pure fancy on my part, since high stone walls have been built at track level to prevent people or cattle wandering off. 'I can still see it, that viaduct,' the man by the Glaxo laboratories had told me, with a note of wonder in his voice. 'Every time I go down there I imagine it's going to be there like it was before.' But how many (or how few) generations must go by before such things are forgotten?

West of the viaduct the embankment has an ash surface and is easy walking, though some farm underpass bridges have been taken out. At Lartington the line bends south and becomes an unpleasant churned-up road to Cat Castle Quarries, beyond which is the lovely Deepdale, difficult to cross now for the reason stated. After this the track runs parallel with the A67 as far as Bowes, where there stands one of the most haunted places I have visited on any old railway. The green-grey stone of the station buildings there on a dull morning is unphotographable, as is the appearance of the glassless windows with their black empty rooms beyond. The only creatures to use the waiting-room now are cattle, which do not differentiate between seating and toilet areas. The spaces between the platforms are littered with brilliant turquoise fertiliser bags, and fragments of old telegraph poles have been left to rot back into the ground. Loose posts and pieces of metal rattle in the wind, which comes in strong and finger-freezing off the moor. It is very difficult now to conceive of this as a place of communication of any sort.

From Bowes the line curves gently up seven to eight miles of moorland valley from which, as always, you are subtly separated so that the moors remain unthreatening – primordial, yes, but impossible to get lost in. There is a lot of broad gravel-covered embankment giving good views, and cattle graze at intervals. At Stainmore Summit – the col – the line is being absorbed into a road improvement scheme (see p. 33), so that you must, I am very sorry to say, walk along a mile or more of tarmac. After that you are descending to Kirkby Stephen, a journey which I will not try to describe, only heartily recommend.

If it still retained its viaducts and bridges, this line would make a first-rate Pennine crossing for cyclists wanting to avoid both steep gradients and motor traffic. Along it, cyclists would have had a direct link between the industrial areas of County Durham and Teesside, and the Lake District. The route could, indeed, be extended back as far as Darlington on a southern branch, whilst Durham County Council already has in its possession the 15½ mile stretch of line running north east from Barnard Castle to Bishop Auckland, which they do indeed propose to redevelop as a recreational route linking with their several other already converted lines.

(Above left) Bowes station.

(Above) Signal box, Bowes.

(Left) Fence made of sleepers, Bowes. Apart from their reuse in ganger's huts (see the Bridport Railway), sound sleepers were also used again for reinforcing embankments prone to slippage.

(Far left) Truncated western portion of the great viaduct across the Tees, north of Barnard Castle. It was 732' long and 132' high.

(Above) The Tees viaduct: on the far bank is the eastern portion.

(Over) The Valley of Argill Beck, from the railway.

(Top right) Road-over-rail bridge, just before the descent to Kirkby Stephen begins.

(Lower right) Not a line to follow at night: the bridge here, north of Barras, is somewhat absent. Looking north east.

(Far right above) Eastern corner of the Vale of Appleby from the same position as lower right, looking north west.

(Far right below) Approaching Kirkby Stephen station, which lies beyond the second bridge. The station here has been developed into a factory making bobbins for the weaving industry.

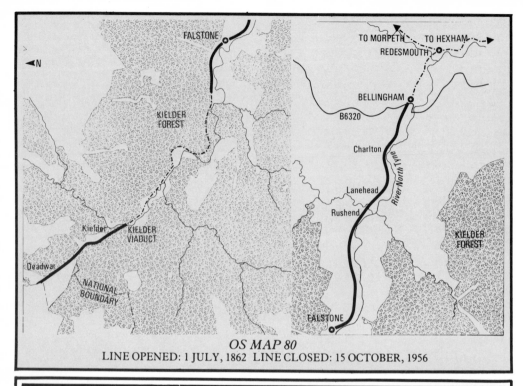

OS MAP 80
LINE OPENED: 1 JULY, 1862 LINE CLOSED: 15 OCTOBER, 1956

THE BORDER COUNTIES RAILWAY

FROM BELLINGHAM TO DEADWATER, NORTHUMBERLAND (20 MILES)

The Border Counties Railway was constructed for the purpose of exploiting the till then unmined North Tyne valley coalfield at Plashetts, and a colliery was started there at the same time as the railway was being built. The line ran its first service on the same day as the North British's Border Union Railway between Hawick and Carlisle opened; the two railways joined a few miles east of the English–Scottish border at Riccarton Junction. For want of industrial buyers for the coal, the railway did not prosper and was speedily taken over by the North British Railway, who obtained running powers over the North Eastern's line from Hexham to Newcastle and began a through passenger service between Edinburgh and Newcastle – a slow, winding, through passenger service: when it started, the fastest journey was 4 hours and 50 minutes, and an evening train that stopped at every station took 6½ hours, arriving at the convenient time of 01.10 a.m. Meantime the Plashetts coal, now being transported to the Tweed towns in the north, proved inadequate for industrial purposes, though it was put to domestic use. The railway found an alternative and unexpected source of income, however, from the shipping of livestock out of and into the Newcastle market.

By 1981 between six and seven miles of the Border Counties Railway will have disappeared under the waters of the new Kielder reservoir. Kielder Water will be three quarters the area of Lake Windermere, and one of the largest artificial lakes in Europe. I decided to explore this line because I thought it would be useful to make some record of the section to be flooded, and also because the railway runs over the border into Scotland, and out of my allotted territory.

In the event, the Bellingham end proved the more rewarding. The railway is far from forgotten there, and evidence of its presence can be found amongst other places in one of the pubs, where a sign behind the bar reads:

> 'Rose and Crown Halt
> Stop Look and Listen
> B. Railway Co.
> Sgd. Sid Allen Gen. Manager.'

In the village cafe, my enquiry after the railwaymen in the area produced a spontaneous outbreak of random reminiscences from the customers, and from each new person that entered. Clearly Bellingham had owed a lot to its railway. I was told the usual stories: how you could get to Edinburgh and back in a day, or to Newcastle on a Saturday night leaving at 4 and arriving back at 1 in the morning; how the Geordies would come up on a 1s. 9d. day return to visit Hareshaw Linn, a local beauty spot; how Bill Cohen of Falstone played the pipes to the last train out of Falstone station. But as to old railwaymen – 'They're all dead,' said one stout lady, as I rather expected that she would, and laughed heartily. 'It's ma' sense o' humour,' she explained. 'No, but what about Willy Scott, wasn't it, used to live down by the station yard?' 'Is *he* still alive?'

Billy Scott was still very much alive, a coal man, then fireman, then storeman at Redesmouth depot between 1920 and 1954, when the engine shed there closed. Twenty five years later his pride in the standards of appearance, and labour, that had existed then was not diminished. 'The shed was a palace,' he told me; he kept the steps to it whitewashed, army-style. His job was as tough as any, especially in winter. He would have to rise at 4 in the morning to get the locos ready for a 7.30 start, and always put a saucer of water on his bedroom window during the cold months to keep a check on the temperature: if it froze, he would get up even earlier in order to light the fires necessary to defrost the water in the engines. Walking the three to four miles between Bellingham and Redesmouth, where on arrival he would also have to rouse the fireman, he would often find that his face was covered with ice: little wonder that he feels bitter about the tiny settlement that British Rail made him on his enforced retirement.

At Bellingham itself, the railway's most important function was transport for the 'Bellingham mart', where sheep are still sold today, and livestock would arrive in trainloads of 30 to 40 wagons, pulled by two locomotives. The roads between the railway and the mart field would be crammed from side to side and end to end with sheep. 'What a mess they used to be in!' Mrs Scott remembered. 'And the little lads would love to get a stick and help to keep the animals moving.' Now, of course, the livestock travels the roads of Bellingham's country not on foot but in lorries; the traders arrive by car, go straight to the mart field, and generally stay away from Bellingham itself, so that community and trade have become separated. The railway also carried livestock from points back up the line towards Hawick into Newcastle for its market, and military horses were taken into Scotland via Hawick for use by the artillery. There was also, glorious thought, a 'whisky train' that ran through Redesmouth carrying large quantities of the water of life from Edinburgh to Newcastle. One wonders what kind of temptation *that* might have offered to the storeman, if a train happened to get halted at Redesmouth overnight!

Billy Scott, a servant of the railway which in his time brought mobility in the shape of six passenger trains per day to this remote area of England, is now dependent upon the local bus service. If he wanted he could still get into Newcastle by train – so long as he first caught the bus to Hexham, sixteen miles south along a motor road winding laboriously down the Tyne valley, in parallel to his railway.

In the old days he and his wife lived in one of a row of cottages opposite the station – these were owned by the Duke of Northumberland, and are now replaced by council houses – and they told the time by the station clock. In the old days, Redesmouth engine shed might have had thirteen or fourteen engines in it, during a busy period. 'But now all that's gone,' said Billy Scott, 'and it's a damned shame.'

(The section of line running south from Redesmouth to High Carry House is now a public path.)

(Top left) Charlton. The line winds up the North Tyne valley; seen from a road crossing, now embanked.

(Bottom left) Lanehead, cutting and ganger's hut.

(Above) Rushend level crossing and crossing-keeper's house.

There are times, as you are walking old railways –

when it seems almost as if –

you yourself may have become a locomotive . . .

(Left) The Kielder reservoir, under construction.

(Lower left) Inside the reservoir site: the line is being used as a haul road.

(Below) Looking towards Plashetts. All this will soon be under water, up to the tree line.

(Bottom) Remains of railway buildings at Plashetts. Everything must be razed to the ground before flooding commences.

(Left) Kielder viaduct (1862), preserved in 1969 by the Northumberland and Newcastle Society, and now to be maintained by the Water Authority. A plaque states that the viaduct is the 'finest surviving example of the skew arch form of construction . . .' whereby '. . . each stone in the arch should be individually shaped in accordance with the method evolved by Peter Nicholson of Newcastle-upon-Tyne, a pioneer geometrician in this field.'

(Above) End of the line in England. The author, photographed by himself, walks over the Scottish border at Deadwater.

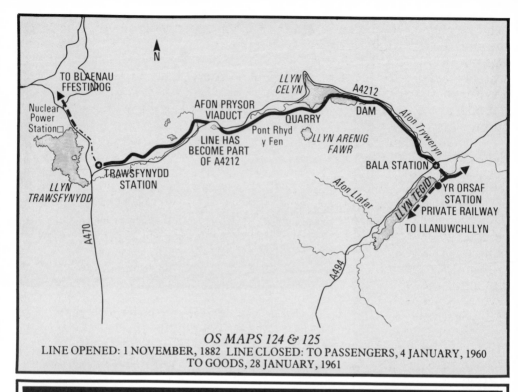

OS MAPS 124 & 125
LINE OPENED: 1 NOVEMBER, 1882 LINE CLOSED: TO PASSENGERS, 4 JANUARY, 1960
TO GOODS, 28 JANUARY, 1961

THE BALA AND FESTINIOG RAILWAY

FROM BALA TO TRAWSFYNYDD, GWYNEDD (16 MILES)

In the days when this railway started, Ffestiniog was spelt by the founding company with one 'f', for the easier comprehension, one would guess, of English gentlemen who had money to put into railway building. The line was no less than the fourth to reach Blaenau Ffestiniog (it did so in two sections, the Ffestiniog to Blaenau Ffestiniog section being completed the earlier, in 1868) with the intention of providing a more direct and competitive route between the slate quarries surrounding the town and the industrial Midlands. At Arenig there were sidings for a hundred wagons to serve a busy granite quarry which is still in operation today, though the quarry works is now sited squarely across the railway trackbed (see p. 30). An artillery camp was opened at Trawsfynydd in 1903, and the station was equipped with a troop yard with its own long platforms. Troop trains were generally run double-

214

headed, and special instructions called for an experienced guard, who knew the line well, to be always placed in charge of them. At the end of its life a fight was put up by some local people to save the line, despite the fact that it was scarcely being used by that time, but re-routing round the then-named Tryweryn reservoir (now Llyn Celyn), would have cost another million pounds, and could not be justified to the satisfaction of the Liverpool Corporation, who would have had to foot the bill.

The track can be followed up the lower reaches of the Afon Tryweryn from Bala (where in the reverse view from the picture of the station site it is perfectly visible in its cutting), running parallel to the A4212 for 3½ miles, at which point the embankment is crossed by a new, private road and you find yourself in the grounds of the pumping station at Llyn Celyn, with a massive dam embankment filling your view. This section could usefully be redeveloped as a footpath link between Bala and Llyn Celyn: at present it seems that everyone who goes there goes by car, and sits in the car park.

Near the point where it comes into the air again I chatted to a lady in what was a hillside, and is now a lakeside, farm. Her family had farmed there for several generations, and she had clear recollections of what the drowned valley had been like, and of the railway, which she remembered with affection. Before the halt had been established by the farm in 1931 she and the other children had had a three mile walk to the station in order to catch the train to school in Bala, but on the way home the driver would often halt in the cutting just beneath the farm, where the pause would not be noticed, and drop them off there. The railwaymen were more than ready to do the locals favours: she told me how they had carried up supplies of 'barm, what you call it, yeast,' for the baking when it was locally unavailable. A longer cutting, a few hundred yards west, had proved an obstacle in winter, and trains regularly got stuck there in the snow; one, she remembered, for a whole week. An attractive little cast-iron bridge remains here, carrying a farm road across the cutting: embossed lettering states that it was cast in Brymbo, near Wrexham, in 1880.

The line continues along the bleak upper valley of the Afon Tryweryn past Arenig, and is uninterrupted as far as Llyn Tryweryn, a natural lake standing at the highest point in the valley, where the river has its source. Here the railway disappears for a short length under the newly engineered A4212, but continues immediately on the other side of the lake, crossing the Cwm Prysor viaduct and then running directly along the steep northern slope of the valley of Afon Prysor as it drops to Llyn Trawsfynydd.

Of all the disused railways I have explored, this section has impressed me the most strongly from the point of view of the immense physical effort that must have been necessary to build it. The line runs high along the steep mountain face, giving a buzzard's view of the world beneath, with the road traffic running prosaically along the valley floor. It alternates between cuttings incised through the mountain's black flank and towering, steep-sided embankments, or bridges spanning waterfall-streams that slide almost vertically down the rock face. How can we conceive fully, now, in an age of instant earth-moving by bulldozers and graders, of the physical difficulties involved in making this vertiginous way with only man- and horse-power? These products of the servants of the B&FR Company remain, for those who choose to see them in this way, as mute testimony to their labours – the cuttings, at least, as indestructible as the pyramids.

The line served its purpose, for seventy-nine years. Yet, here in particular, this does not seem enough. Such engineering was surely worth far more than a mere seventy-nine years of operation. How could it be reused now? By a preservation society, perhaps? No services will ever come up here from Bala, the most obvious terminus, unless some operator finds a way of running locomotives underwater. Why not, then, as a cycleway and footpath, with perhaps a link path around the south side of Llyn Celyn, joining the broken halves of the line together once more? The Afon Prysor valley section is a hill-walker's dream – an easy path along the length of a near-vertical mountainside: it is, in particular, an exhausted hill-walker's dream. It could be a path linking Bala lake and the reservoirs of Celyn and Trawfynydd. But no such plan exists.

(Right) Bala: site of the road-over-rail bridge. The railway ran to the right of the conifers at left of frame. The rail station has been supplanted by a fire station, and the bridge replaced by a solid embankment. The rest of the station yard is redeveloped as an industrial estate. The goods shed here was disguised as a castle, with turrets, to pacify a local landowner who opposed the railway. Looking south east.

(Above) The point at which the railway emerges from the waters of Llyn Celyn. About two miles of track are submerged. Looking north east.

(Left) The cutting where the train stopped unofficially to drop the local children off, now a few hundred yards south of the reservoir.

(*Above*) *Not only the railway has died here. Arenig.*

(*Right*) *Pont-Rhyd-y-Fen, looking east. Anyone searching for the Sublime (in the eighteenth-century sense) should not be disappointed if he walks a disused Welsh mountain line on a gloomy day.*

(Above left) The curved arch viaduct over Afon Prysor from the south . . .

(Above) . . . and from the north. Viaducts are arguably the most important relics of the old railway network now remaining in the landscape. They redefine the places around them in their own terms, adding to them rather than damaging them. This stretch of anonymous mountain moorland becomes exhilarating precisely because of the presence of the viaduct.

(Below left) Farmer's underpass, one mile west of the Afon Prysor viaduct.

(Above far left) Embankment and bridge from beneath Craig Aderyn.

(Left) Embankment and cutting, Craig Aderyn, looking east.

(Top) Closer view of cutting.

(Above right) Trawsfynydd station, weighbridge in foreground.

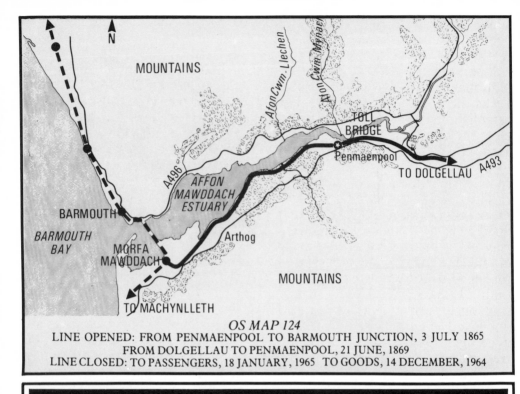

OS MAP 124
LINE OPENED: FROM PENMAENPOOL TO BARMOUTH JUNCTION, 3 JULY 1865
FROM DOLGELLAU TO PENMAENPOOL, 21 JUNE, 1869
LINE CLOSED: TO PASSENGERS, 18 JANUARY, 1965 TO GOODS, 14 DECEMBER, 1964

THE DOLGELLAU BRANCH

FROM PENMAENPOOL TO MORFA MAWDDACH, GWYNEDD (5 MILES)

This lovely stretch of line was taken over by the Cambrian Railway in a half-completed state from the Aberystwyth and Welsh Coast Railway Company; the second section of the line was then built to link up at Dolgellau with the Great Western's route from north west England, and the tourist passengers it carried. The Cambrian Railway had their own route to the north west, running over a far greater number of miles than the Great Western line, through Machynlleth and Welshpool, and in constructing this link they were evidently hedging their bets. If Great Western did prove to be the company carrying the bulk of the holidaymakers, then at least the Cambrian Railway would be able to take them over the last few miles to Barmouth and the coast. When, about fifty years after it opened, Great Western finally took over the branch, they carried out some rebuilding at Dolgellau station, and moved the single platform at Penmaenpool to its present position. Great Western advertised the trip to the Welsh coast as 'one of the most enchanting in the world,' and they may quite possibly have been right.

The section I walked is now an official path in the care of Snowdonia National Park, and was in the process of being surfaced with a fine shale when I was there. At Penmaenpool, the George Hotel was once a boat-builder's establishment. If you sit on one of the benches outside you are aware how close the line ran to the building, perhaps no more than five or six feet from it at the closest point. The boat builders must have needed to pay close attention to the railway timetable in order to survive. Now the line here functions as a road to the pub car park, which is on the site of the engine shed.

The straight section of embankment west of Penmaenpool gives what is, to me, a very satisfying separation from the surrounding marshland fields, with a good clear view at every point. For anyone who has ever tried to make their way along the winding, muddy paths of estuary marshes the man-made efficiency of this engineered route is striking by contrast. I met a farmer on the marsh who seemed perfectly happy about the fact that the railway was now a path. He agreed that though now it was open people could cross land where previously there had been no right of way of any sort, by its nature as a fenced and gated embankment the line allowed free passage without pedestrians ever needing to enter any of the fields. His one concern was that some might trespass off it and take their dogs into fields where sheep were grazing. It would be useful to note whether that kind of destructive action does markedly increase in places where old lines have been opened up for access. I very much doubt that it will.

This section of line does make a fine walk, enabling the unpowered traveller to get right to the edge of the Afon Mawddach estuary where previously the only way to see it from this angle was – to travel by train. The main road running parallel to the south is cut off by hills and woods and affords only tantalising glimpses of the water. There is, as with all the best walking, a satisfying feeling here of being rewarded for one's efforts: it takes a while to get to the estuary, but once you are there you can be certain that no cars, or lorries, or motorcycles, will get between you and the beauty of the place. Only the faint sound of traffic from the main road on the north side of the water, occasionally audible beyond the piping of oyster-catchers and the cawing of rooks, qualifies the impression of wilderness.

(Above far left) The line from the A493, Foel Ispri beyond.

(Below far left) Stone facing to embankment, Penmaenpool.

(Centre left) Looking east along the line from the George Hotel.

(Centre below left) Signal box, Penmaenpool.

(Left) Penmaenpool: the toll bridge over the Afon Mawddach.

(Below) Station house, Penmaenpool.

(Right) This embankment across marshy fields gives the walker a driver's view of the landscape, leading you forwards in a dead straight line for about a mile until you reach the water's edge.

(Above) Same section, looking east. The sea came over here in 1977, spreading the ballast.

(Left) From a point just over a mile west of Penmaenpool the line continues along the water's edge.

(Top) A private garage in the village of Arthog.

(Above) Morfa Mawddach: junction of live and dead lines. This junction was called Barmouth Junction until 1960.

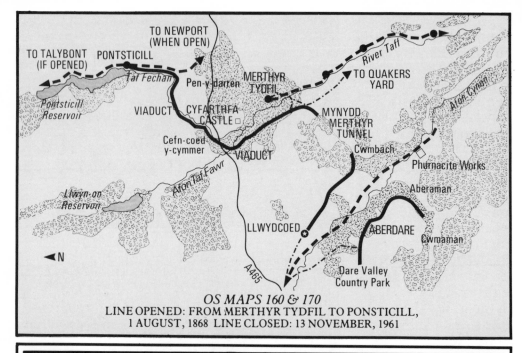

OS MAPS 160 & 170
LINE OPENED: FROM MERTHYR TYDFIL TO PONTSTICILL,
1 AUGUST, 1868 LINE CLOSED: 13 NOVEMBER, 1961

THE BRECON AND MERTHYR TYDFIL JUNCTION RAILWAY, AMONGST OTHERS

FROM LLWYDCOED, MID GLAMORGAN TO PONTSTICILL STATION, POWYS (10½ MILES)

The disused railways of the South Wales mining valleys, like those of South Yorkshire and County Durham, are stranded across the Ordnance Survey maps in such profusion that on first sight they seem as if they must have grown along the valleys with all the insensate arbitrariness of a convolvulus. Yet, rightly or wrongly, railway historians generally give the impression that there were perfectly good reasons at the time for the establishment of each and every route. My intended journey began at Llwydcoed, one of the station towns of the link line between Merthyr Tydfil and the Vale of Neath railway, which was amalgamated with Great Western in 1865. I intended to join up with the Merthyr Branch running to Pontsticill, either by walking through the tunnel under Mynydd Merthyr or, if that proved impossible, by going around the mountain and meeting up with the line on the other side.

However, in my exploration of this stretch I also ambled over to the other side of the Cynon valley to take a brief look at the remains of the railway running through Aberaman and into Aberdare and beyond (this line does in fact branch to connect with what was the Vale of Neath Railway, at the same point that the Merthyr branch also joins it). Now, in Aberaman, the line is a central pedestrian artery made by common usage but eventually to be officialised along the whole length from Cwmaman to Aberdare, and serves the sprawl of houses that runs around the hillside there. From a bridge near the town centre you can look directly down one of many grim, steep streets and begin to make some sense out of the chaos of development in the valley bottom: you can see how the industry supplanted valley farms and mines sprang up along the hillsides, how what were villages grew along the roads and up the slopes, how the fields were excavated or dumped upon and are now, in places, being reclaimed as parks and sports areas. It seems that the very mountains here might be piles of slag. On the other side of the valley the area below the Merthyr link line at Cwmbach was used for tipping coal waste, and people still scratch below the thin grass to glean fuel for their fires. From either railway you are looking down into the industrialised, urbanised valley, at the whitish haze of aerial pollution from the phurnacite works which hangs like a heavy mist, ending at approximately the height that the habitation also ends. Here is a landscape in which the history of the exploitation of both men and environment is laid out diagrammatically, as if in a child's drawing; and from the dead railways which were once instrumental in this landscape's growth the diagram has even greater clarity.

The tunnel under Mynydd Merthyr, like the monumental Cefn Coed viaduct, is another of those pieces of railway engineering which forces you to think of the appalling waste involved in closure. Here is a tunnel puncturing through the centre of a mountain to link two valleys, and no-one is using it for anything, except to write messages on the wall for other idle adventurers to read, or ignore, or add to. The tunnel has apparently been considered for use in transporting coal recovered from the Cwmbach tip to Merthyr, but nothing actual has come of these considerations.

Originally British Rail blocked the entrance, but the barricade was subsequently vandalised so they took it down again, which means that here you can indeed walk right in, if you so choose. Entering a railway tunnel where trains no longer run is a disturbing experience. It has been said that in our imaginations we die whenever we pass through a tunnel by train, and wait in suspense for the rebirth at the other end; but by foot, at four miles per hour if that, the rebirth is a long time in coming. You listen to your footsteps echoing, beyond the crunching of the ballast, deep into the black recesses of the mountain. You think, perhaps, of how many might have died in blasting this hole through the rock. Water drips in the shadows – but is it water, you may wonder, or is it the whisperings of malevolent troglodytic creatures waiting there to drag you, screaming uselessly (for who is there to hear?) down into the dark? And what if you were to find, at the far end of the tunnel, that a brick barrier stands there, impassable? Your stomach tightens, your breathing becomes strained and heavy. What was that, there – something moving? I walked – I think – about four hundred yards into the Merthyr tunnel before I turned round and briskly made my way back, with no self-apologies, to the exit. Later I met a local man who had braved the whole length of the same tunnel with two friends when he was a boy. There was just one difference about his experience: at that time the railway was operational, and they were very nearly hit by a train, only avoiding it by crushing themselves back against the tunnel wall, since they could not find a refuge in time. 'It scared me, I can tell you,' he said. I quite understood his feelings.

From Merthyr to Pontsticill and beyond the line was established by what D. S. Barrie, in his 1957 book on the subject, calls a 'vigorous, if virtually insolvent, little terrier of a railway', the Brecon and Merthyr, from whose main line (opened 1 January 1863) the stretch to Merthyr town was a branch. The construction of the viaducts at Pontsarn and Cefn Coed was the direct result of the strategically necessary re-routing of the line to avoid a local stately home, Cyfarthfa Castle, in order to win the support of its influential occupants. This castle is now almost entirely surrounded by the suburbs of Merthyr Tydfil. Another problem stemming from this re-routing was that the descent from Pontsticill was steep, an almost continuous 1 in 45–50, and two complete reversals of direction were necessary on each journey. The opening of the branch legally enabled the Brecon and Merthyr Railway Company to go on to complete its through route from Brecon to Newport and, eventually, to pull itself out of the familiar financial hot water – with, in this case, the rolling stock having been vested in the directors on trust for numerous creditors in order to allow services to continue at all. Merthyr was at the time one of those towns that all the railway companies wanted to get a wheel-hold in and, after the London and North Western Railway had put a great deal of pressure on the B&MRC, the two companies ran the Merthyr branch jointly: the B&M recovered from the L&NW half the cost of construction, at twenty-five thousand Victorian pounds per mile.

The embankment west of Merthyr is itself a long, thin slag heap made out of quarrying and mining waste. Again here it has not taken official designation for the railway to be useful to the local community; it is clearly very much in use as a footpath. The riverbank beneath the Cefn Coed viaduct is also much used by walkers – there is a public footpath here, though not beneath the viaduct itself, where most people seem to go, and the place has become a 'beauty spot' precisely because this superlative piece of nineteenth-century design stands there, *curving* from one side of the valley to the other. You wonder, looking at it, whether it would stand as long as the Roman aqueduct at Segovia, for example, given the right help at the right times. The viaduct is now in the hands of Merthyr Tydfil Borough Council, as is the Pontsarn viaduct: both have been registered as Class II listed buildings, which is encouraging. The council are 'currently considering' the problems of maintenance and public usage.

At Pontsticill station, the junction of the Merthyr branch and the Brecon and Merthyr's also disused Newport route, a new private railway is being set up. The owner, Mr. A. J. Hills, plans initially to run services southwards along a two-mile stretch of the Newport line, after which the railway will extend north along the Pontsticill reservoir. The line could in time run as far north as Talybont, in the Usk valley. Mr. Hills has been told that he could run his trains down the Merthyr branch too if he wanted – provided, of course, that he took over the responsibilities of maintenance on the two viaducts.

(Right) Aberaman. The line is now in use as a footpath. Looking north east.

(Above far right) Aberaman: a barrier no longer necessary, at least from the railway's point of view.

(Below far right) The Cynon valley, dominated by the phurnacite works. Looking south east from Aberaman.

(Above) *Entrance to the Merthyr tunnel, north of Cwmbach. The tunnel, over a mile long, runs north east under Mynydd Merthyr to link the Cynon and Taff valleys.*

(Right) *Post-industrial landscape: the railway is one only of many artefacts abandoned here by industries that no longer required them. Looking south east.*

(Far right) *West of Merthyr Tydfil, looking south east. About a mile from this spot, at Pen-y-darren, the first steam locomotive capable of drawing a load over rails was operated in February 1804.*

(Right) *Chucked away, like an old Coke can: the Cefn Coed viaduct, running across the Afon Taf Fawr valley at Cefn-Coed-y-Cymmer, seen from the south east. It is a 15-bay structure, 770' long, completed in 1866.*

(Above) *The new road bridge, seen from the Cefn Coed viaduct: the later design for bridging the valley is certainly more economic in materials, but is it as impressive? Will it be looked upon with awe by future generations?*

(*Above and opposite*) *The Cefn Coed viaduct.*

(*Above right*) *Pontsticill: the beginnings of a new private narrow-gauge railway. The locomotive is an 0-6-2 tender tank, built by Arn Jung in 1908 and used in Mecklenburg. Nineteen other locomotives are on order and awaiting road transport to Pontsticill station.*

(*Below right*) *The Pontsarn viaduct, across the Taf Fechan at Faenor. Looking south east.*

THE LAST RESTING PLACE

No exploration of disused railways would be complete without some mention of the mausoleums into which disused locomotives and rolling stock are taken to await dismantling, either for reusable parts or for scrap.

Rolling stock has, of course, been simply dumped along some disused lines . . .

. . . or has been put into makeshift farm use:

On the Merthyr branch, west of Merthyr Tydfil.

Near Stottesdon, on the Ditton Priors branch. Sleepers in the foreground; the wagon has been used for storing hay.

But most rolling stock finds its way, along with the locomotives, into a yard such as British Rail's unfortunately named Concentration Yard (shortened to 'Con Yard' by railway workers) at Swindon. Here parts which can be reused are removed. . . .

A diesel engine awaiting dismantling.

. . . and the hulks are cut up in situ, so that the pieces can be taken away by scrap merchants.

Sleeper indeed.

Sleeping & Messing Coach
For use with Steam Crane № 2
CM&EEs Department SWINDON

At Barry Island in South Glamorgan is sited a scrapyard, known to every steam preservationist in the country: it is operated by Woodham Bros., railway dismantlers. Between the late 1950s and 1967 when the last consignment arrived there, the yard was used as a collecting point for the many hundreds of steam locomotives from all regions which had been made redundant by British Railways as the changeover to diesel and electric power took place. The locomotives and stock were intended for scrapping, and many have been dismantled – the metal being reused, amongst other purposes, for the manufacture of cars and aircraft. However as a result of the upsurgence of steam preservation societies, a number of the locomotives at the Woodham Bros. yard have been saved from dismemberment: the first to be restored was a Midland 4F 0-6-0 freight locomotive no 43924, purchased in 1968 by the Midland 4F Preservation Society. Since then over 80 other locos have been sold, and most of these have now left the yard. It seems unlikely that many of the remainder can be preserved, and so the hulks stand amongst the rose bay willow herb, rusted to a deep russet red, awaiting the arrival of the men with the oxyacetylene torches. The yard is no longer open to the general public.

A wagon being dismantled.

Wagon wheels awaiting removal.

Scrap and more scrap. But the locomotives have purchasers, or would-be purchasers.

What chance is there that any driver will again see a moving landscape through this window?

More than a fighting chance for this loco, the 7828 'Odney Manor', which used to run on the Cambrian Coast Express from Shrewsbury to Aberystwyth and was scrapped in the early sixties. It awaits collection by the society that has saved it.

PART FOUR
PUBLIC ACCESS TO DISUSED RAILWAYS

'Progress be damned! All this will do is to allow the lower classes to move around unnecessarily.'
Attributed to Arthur Wellesley, Duke of Wellington, at the time of the debates preceding the passing of the Great Western Railway Bill on August 31, 1835.

WHAT MIGHT HAVE BEEN . . .

Imagine, if you will, a network of broad interconnecting trackways running across Britain, which are physically separated from all forms of motor traffic; trackways available only to those who travel without the artificial aid of the internal combustion engine, using their own energy or that of animals – walkers, cyclists, or equestrians; trackways joining East Anglia with Wales,

255

and Hampshire with Scotland, and linked where necessary by judicious re-routing of their traffic along bridleways, footpaths or back lanes; trackways running unhindered and uninterrupted out of the centres of our metropolitan areas, with thin strips of tarmac for cyclists along their most heavily used stretches, enabling inhabitants to leave without being poisoned by a single cloud of petrol fumes, and connecting the depressed inner city areas directly with the open land. Imagine that such 'greenways' had been planted with sturdy trees like beech, chestnut, and oak, and that these had by now begun to mature so that the routes led out across the landscape like Napoleon's avenues in France, lined with poplars for the shelter of his marching armies; imagine that in hilly places the tracks had been edged with sweet-scented Scots pines, in others with the monumental dark masses of copper beech, in others with the silver-leafed aspen, that this planting continued uninterrupted into the centres of urban areas, and that the routes were most carefully tended where they were most obviously needed, in the areas where vandalism was rife. Imagine all viaducts, all bridges, all tunnels on these ways intact and well maintained by local councils under the central administration of a 'Greenway Authority'. Finally, imagine that – as the petrol ran out – some of these ways were made to function again in society, because the provident administration had kept them open as through routes, if not as railways then as ways for some newly devised, more economic form of mass transport.

This map attempts no more than an approximate representation of its subject. Short lengths are omitted, and where many disused lines are located near to one another (as for example in South Wales) it is even further simplified. Lines which are still in use for any railway purpose, even if it is only for the most meagre goods traffic, are not included.

Roughly two thirds of the lines were closed in or after 1963: in some areas, for example the West Country, post-Beeching closures account for almost all the lines shown. If the Beeching-closed lines only had been preserved we could now be benefiting from greenways running, for example, between the Dorset coast and the Quantock Hills in Somerset (the Somerset and Dorset line), between the south western suburban belt of Greater London and the south coast (the Guildford to Shoreham-by-Sea line), or between the industrial zone of South Wales and the Breconshire and Radnorshire mountains (the railways running from Swansea to Llanidloes and Presteigne). If you study this map with the aid of the atlases mentioned in the bibliography you can compose your own route – in theory, if not in practise.

It is also worth pointing out that many of the pre-Beeching closures are even now still intact for long stretches: in 1963 they were of course far more intact, since the vast majority of such closures occurred only in the '50s or early '60s. Combining the Beeching and pre-Beeching closures, the bases for greenways between East Anglia and Wales, and Hampshire and Scotland, are not difficult to discern.

This, then, was the resource available to us. If you compare this map with that on page 278 you will have some idea of what, for recreational and straightforward pedestrian purposes, we have so far made of it.

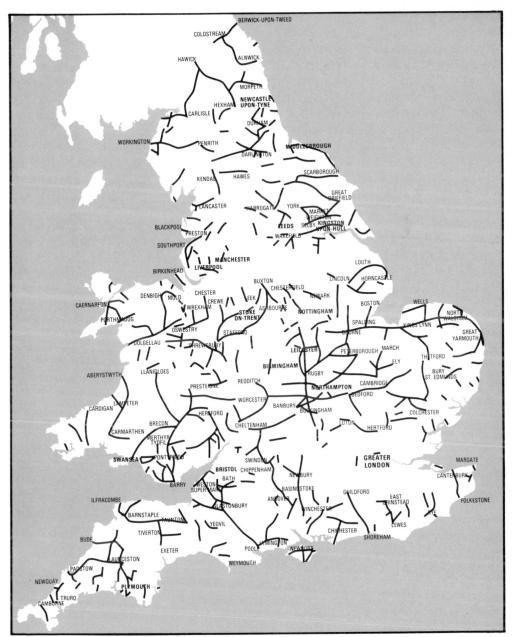

THE DISUSED RAILWAYS OF ENGLAND AND WALES

In contrast with such an absolute ideal as this, the actual reuse of disused railways today is little short of pathetic. The big question, of course, is whether such an ideal was from the start unattainable. I do not think so. It would not have been unattainable if there had been as much as a single man of vision there in a position of responsibility to fight for it, if not from the time of nationalisation onwards, then at least from 1963, the year of the Beeching Report. Remember that disused railway lines were in the hands of a nationalised industry directly responsible to central government: the through routes *were all there*, intact and readily workable, in government hands. But what did government do, via British Rail, neé British Railways? It sold the routes off, in little bits and pieces, to whoever could find the cash and would also agree to take over the responsibilities of maintenance. British Rail was and is under statutory obligation to offer disused lines first of all to the local authorities in whose areas they are situated; the local authority then has six weeks (in terms of council decision-making processes, of course, an absurdly short length of time) to state whether it wants the land or not, after which, if the answer is 'no thanks', it can be sold to first comers. This obligation on its own is not enough: since very many authorities had absolutely no concept of recreational reuse of railway land in the early stages of the Beeching closures, and even if

(*Above*) *Going, going . . . This is at Castle Hedingham, Essex. Two miles ahead a short section of line is in use by the Colne Valley Railway Company.*

they had could readily argue against taking on the responsibility because they could not justify the expense or work involved in the service of 'minority groups' (cyclists and only a few walkers being thought likely to use the remoter stretches), the answer was very often 'no thanks'. The result is that the continuity of all disused lines has been speedily and relentlessly broken. And, therefore, all subsequent attempts to restore them as through routes has had to be undertaken retroactively, *undoing* the destructive work of the procedure of sale. In certain cases the local authorities themselves have been confronted with broken routes which, in retrospect, they would have much preferred unbroken: Cheshire County Council's Wirral Country Park, for example, is broken in two places by District Council housing estates which are now regarded as 'inconvenient obstacles', (Information sheet on the Country Park.)

At the same time that they are obliged to offer the land to local authorities, British Rail also have a statutory duty to sell for as good a price as they can get. It is worthwhile considering the implications of this . Not only does it mean that once the local authority has made its refusal the route can be broken into scores of fragments by sale to private individuals, but that the recouping of money must be the prime object of the Property Board's sales activities, no matter what other plans are put forward. When, for example, the National Trust approached British Rail with exemplary promptness in 1963 with a view to taking over certain routes as walks, it was made clear from the outset that British Rail was not going to so much as consider giving the land to the Trust – which is the only way that the Trust could have got it. The deal was cash, or no deal. Similarly, when Cumbria County Council tried to persuade British Rail to dedicate a right of way along a section of the Barnard Castle–Kirkby Stephen line prior to returning it to agriculture, British Rail refused. Better to sell the land off in little bits and pieces for the relatively paltry sums it would raise, it was evidently believed (and compared to the massive subsidies the railways needed to keep going, especially in the sixties, the receipts from the sale of disused land are but the tiniest drop in the ocean: even today it can be sold for as little as £10 per acre), than to find some way of preserving the routes intact either for the immediate or for the possible long-term public good. After all, there is a statutory obligation to sell, and statutes have to be obeyed. But why were no voices raised in protest? Why was the statute not changed? Could it be, perhaps, that the administration of British Rail had been so steeped in the depressing business of taking things apart that no-one there was capable of projecting the benefits still to be derived from routes now and for all time officially defined as irrelevant superfluities? It may be noted, in this context, that the Leek and Manifold Valley Light Railway path in Derbyshire, which so far as I am aware is the first path to have been made out of a disused railway line, came into being as C. E. M. Joad noted, as a result of 'the benevolent L.M.S., who just before the last war covered it with a tarmac road surface about six feet wide with gates so arranged that only pedestrians could pass through.' This, then, is an example of a commercial railway company helping to institute a change for the betterment of non-railway travellers. When has any similar move been made by the nationalised British Rail?

I have borrowed the term 'greenway' from Michael Dower (son of John Dower, the prime mover in the founding of the English National Parks), whose article 'Green Ways – A Positive Future for Britain's Cast Off Railways?' appeared in the Architectural Review for December 1963, a few months after the Beeching Report was published. Dower argued for a network – for the benefit of walkers, cyclists, and horse riders. He added the 1800 miles of disused canal towpaths, the existing ancient trackways and the projected long-distance paths to the total of closed or to-be-closed railway lines, concluding that what we possessed was 'a formidable reserve of uncommitted linear routes' which could now be creatively exploited. He posited a 5000-mile-long network of paths connecting major centres of population with the national parks and other areas of outstanding beauty, which would also function as a means of linking otherwise fragmentary public rights of way together. On one point only – the segregation of cyclists and horseriders by keeping them to separate railway lines – would I disagree with Dower, since this really is not necessary except in very high pressure areas: if cyclists and equestrians can pass on bending country lanes, they can certainly pass on railway lines. Here was the basis for what could have been a magnificent development in the liberation of Technological Man from his machines. Dower estimated that at that time it would cost around £500,000 to purchase 5000 miles of disused railway, which equals about 2½ old pence per head of population, and that the subsequent maintenance of the entire network would be around £50,000 per annum. This was certainly an underestimate, especially in the figure for maintenance, but even if the costs had been ten times higher it would have been worth finding the money, considering the long-term benefits to be had.

The article also suggested that the National Parks Commission should designate the tracks as long-distance paths, and that they should subsequently be administered by local authorities, with a 100 per cent grant for construction and maintenance. But who listened to these suggestions? Evidently, no-one. The £500,000+ was not found, and British Rail went on hawking bits of line, for as much as it could get, to people who wanted to live in old station buildings and grow cabbages on the trackbed (which is in itself not at all a bad idea). The National Parks Commission did not do any designating; though it should be remembered that 1963 was two years before the first long distance path was officially established and therefore that the precedent for any long-distance recreation route had yet to be set. Even so, once it *had* been set, why was this other 'formidable reserve' not immediately tapped?

As David St. John Thomas observes in 'The Country Railway' (pages 165–6), 'the railways popularised the country as well as opening it up. Hundreds of thousands of slum dwellers who may have missed out on the finer points of hill and valley scenery none the less sooner or later breathed country air and found some new dimension to life,' and 'from around the turn of the century for little more than a week's wages an averagely paid Birmingham skilled worker might visit Yarmouth, Weston-super-Mare, Llandridnod Wells, Morecambe and Grassington in a single season . . .' 'Glaswegians could . . . reach England's south coast.' The working classes, or some of them, did indeed 'move around unnecessarily.'

Glaswegians could have continued to reach England's south coast – along *disused* railways; and, except for the initial outlay on equipment, the transport would have cost them nothing more than the price of the extra supply of blood sugar, in the form of dates or Kendal Mint Cake, necessary to keep the wheels turning or the boots moving one in front of the other. If working railways acted as a liberating influence for the underprivileged, disused railways could have continued this function for those unable – or unwilling – to own a car, and those not sufficiently rich (I am amongst them) to afford the phantasmagoric prices now charged by British Rail on its Inter-city lines.

On June 22nd, 1935, an article by Tom Stephenson appeared in the 'Daily Herald' in which he proposed a 'faint line on the Ordnance Maps which the feet of grateful pilgrims would, with the passing years, engrave on the face of the land.' Stephenson (no relation, unfortunately for my argument, to the Stephenson of the 'Rocket'), who later became secretary of the Ramblers' Association, was here proposing for the first time the creation of a 'Pennine Way from the Peak to the Cheviots.' He had a lot more proposing to do after that: the first long-distance footpath was not opened until thirty years later, in April 1965, after battle beyond battle. It is estimated that up to 10,000 people per annum now attempt the full, difficult 250-mile length of the Pennine Way: the grateful pilgrims did indeed flock to the new route. Other long-distance paths followed, under the aegis of the Countryside Commission: the

Pembrokeshire Coast Path was opened in 1970, the Offa's Dyke Path in 1971, the South Downs Way in 1972 – in all twelve routes are approved, if not yet completely opened. The paths are defined in a current leaflet on them as 'national routes with continuous rights of way offering opportunities for *walkers, horse riders, or cyclists to make extensive journeys that mostly avoid roads used by motor traffic*,' (my italics). In many instances, the rights of way (and attendant track, beaten earth, stiles, gates, etc.) for the long-distance foot-paths did not exist beforehand: they had to be created specially – the paths were not, in fact, through routes until they were made so by local negotiation. *Railways* were never through routes, until this was achieved by local negotia-tion: after which they continued to exist as such even when disused (with certain rare exceptions in which the railway property automatically reverted to the ownership of specific landowners or estates as a result of contractual agreements at the time of construction) until they were sold off.

A pity, then, that Tom Stephenson or his like could not have been on the right committees at the right time, to take up Michael Dower's suggestions and argue for a similar reuse for disused railways. A pity, for that matter, that C. E. M. Joad was not around (he died in 1953): in his book 'The Untutored Townsman's Invasion of the Country' (1946), he gleefully confesses to tres-passing down still-working railways, arguing with some reason that it was a lot safer walking along a quiet branch line than along a traffic-infested main road. Amongst the lines he walked were Parracombe to Lynmouth in Devon, Penrhyndeudraeth to Blaenau Ffestiniog in Meirionnydd, and Pulborough to Midhurst in Sussex. He argued that for the safety and sanity of the populace the law should be reversed for certain major roads (thus it would become illegal to walk or cycle on these roads – c.f. the existing laws on motorways today), and for certain railways so that 'a number of single line railway tracks which are rapidly falling into disuse should be set aside for walkers. The metals should be taken up, the grass allowed to grow and the track trans-formed into a green lane thrown open to the public.' Amongst the examples he gave of lines which could be converted in this way is the Bewdley–Tenbury line in Salop, with its branch to Ditton Priors . . . Alas, as we know, neither along the Ditton Priors branch nor along any other disused line were such recommendations acted upon at that time. 'We spend enough money on motor roads,' writes Joad; 'it is high time that we spent a little on walkers whom motors have displaced.' That little is now being spent, on the long-distance paths and the Recreational Paths which are being provided, usually out of a reorganisation of existing rights of way, by local authorities. But of the twelve long-distance paths only one, the South Downs Way, is open for its full length to horseriders and cyclists; the Ridgeway can be ridden along its western half, and the North Downs Way can be ridden in parts – and even then, the riding is far from easy for cyclists: especially in wet weather the Ridgeway (in my own experience) becomes entirely impassable since its surface turns to glue which instantly fills the mudguards and stops the wheels from turning. The long-distance paths, in truth, offer *realistic* opportunities only to walkers, and to horse-riders only along a certain small percentage of their full length. In the same way only 5 of the 33 Recreational Paths listed in the current leaflet are, to start with, officially open to cyclists and/or horse-riders – and lo and behold, four of these five are converted railway lines! (the Wirral Way, the High Peak Trail, the Tissington Trail, and the Forest Way in East Sussex).

Disused railways – as a rough generalisation based on my explorations of them – are places that people do not want very much. Sections may be wanted for specific purposes; other purposes may be found because the land is sitting there doing nothing, I would guess as often as not in an 'oh well, I suppose we'd better find *some* way of using the thing' frame of mind. Farmers and landowners will sometimes purchase a piece of track running through their land with no more positive plan than to protect themselves by reabsorbing this dangerous incursion route under the totem of Private Property. And mile upon mile upon mile lies utterly unused from year to year.

Yet consider the advantages that the greenway network would have offered to society at large. The 'trespassers' (and people will go on them; debarring notices and barbed wire or not, incursions will be made) would have been given the status of legitimate travellers, able to go far further afield than their present wanderings on the officially opened stretches will allow. They would have then moved along routes solidly separated from farmland by well-maintained railway fences or new hedges (the onus being on the local authority to maintain these); there might well have been a shift of numbers from more destructive country exploration to these routes, where few would have been tempted to trample through the crops except where legitimate paths were indicated, because the railway route was so clearly defined. The clearance of scrub and maintenance of tree growth along the tracks, except at sections designated as nature reserves, again by local authorities taking over the responsibilities of British Rail direct and without interruption, would have inhibited at the start the currently much feared function of now-overgrown railways as 'pest motorways' whereby rabbits, foxes and so on can spread unchecked into areas that were earlier free from them. The separation from roads and road traffic would have allowed mobility even for the young without accidents – when did you last hear of two cyclists, or a cyclist and a horse-rider, crashing? – and the desire of the majority of *motorists* for through routes in places of beauty that are free from *motors* would at last have been satisfied in a much more fundamental way than the provision of car parks round the corner from the place in question. (I am referring here to the findings of researchers in the Peak District Planning Board's 1970 traffic management experiment in the Goyt valley: this is a beauty spot which had been made into an ugliness spot by the hundreds of cars driven to it along an apallingly congested route and then parked all over it. The experiment kept the cars out, and visitors were carried from a car park by free minibuses to the place they had come to visit, which they could then actually see for the first time. Ninety per cent of motorists responding to the questionnaire agreed that the Goyt Valley was enormously improved by the removal of their cars). Sponsored walks, which have indeed been carried out on disused lines – for example on the Kingswinford Branch – and which have been the cause of many serious accidents along motor roads could have been conducted over very long distances without any fear of danger, except perhaps that some walkers might tread on others' toes. Finally, for those who valued railways, the greenways would have existed as the next best thing available, with all major structures intact, as permanent reminders of the full extent of our railway heritage, still accessible for exploration and reflection, if no longer by steam or diesel power.

The walkers' lobby, unfortunately, never did press hard for access to disused railways except in localised instances. What they saw on closure was tracks with ballast well-sterilised by weedkillers, their rails still down and flanked by telegraph posts, the vegetation of the banks still razed in many places by cutting and burning. They saw the long, open vistas and the apparently always boring gentle gradients. They did not think, evidently, that the lines could be utterly transformed, or would transform themselves without human assistance. Even now the Countryside Commission tell me that they would not initiate conversions of viable stretches of track into long-distance paths on behalf of walkers, because they are boring to walk for long distances. The proof of this pudding, of course, must be in the walking: who can be certain, if disused railways were opened over long stretches for whatever purpose, that walkers would not come to use them?

The strongest case for the network, though (and I should say, for whatever fragmentary network is now possible, nearly twenty years too late) the great benefits that it would undoubtedly bring to that now rapidly expanding body of persons who at other times may be 'motorists', or 'articulated lorry drivers', or 'airline pilots', but who choose to get about at least for a part of their lives by bicycle – and of whom some, be it remembered, can afford no other means of transport to the country. What suits the bicycle will also suit the walker and the horserider. In their 1969 paper 'Disused Railway Lines – The Cyclists' Case' (the first section of which is entitled 'An Early Plea', but I am sorry to say – since I am in agreement with every argument contained – that it was, in fact, a rather late plea) The Cyclists' Touring Club put forward a strong case for the creation of special routes for cyclists. In addition to a number of the points I have already raised, the paper stresses the potential value of motor-free cycleways for children: 'the highly valued level of personal mobility enjoyed by the adult population' (in cars) 'has resulted in a corresponding drop in the mobility of children.' In other words, some children riding bicycles get knocked down by cars, and because of this many other children are prevented by their parents from riding at all. One might add to this that the long-term result of the motor-domination of the urban and suburban world must be a drop in the initiative of children, who simply wait for the day they can get their first scooter, graduating via a motorbike to car status, thus remaining perpetually trapped with power machines in the road world, growing inevitably into the rather chubby, rather seedy Mr. and Mrs. Average who drive into the country in their cars with no more exciting or clear-sighted purpose than to find somewhere to park and have a picnic, without *their* children being knocked down by yet further motorists – for these, the 'picnic site' has been created. I must also add that in this context the potential function of the greenway as a route out of urban and metropolitan areas is vitally important. As a cyclist once living in London and regularly riding out of it from near the centre both northwards and southwards, I often dreamed of a route of this sort. How wonderful not to have to slog for one to two hours out of the Heart of Darkness, through the grey grit and unceasing merciless traffic, before you got to real fields! As an adult I was at least able to get out of town by bicycle: but what chance do children in cities have of doing the same? They must wait to be taken, or not go at all. But if there were green routes into cities, entirely free from cars, then the situation would be very different.

The Cyclists' Touring Club paper also illustrates the point that if facilities are made whereby people can propel themselves in safety, there will be no shortage of takers, using as an example the independent cycleway system in Stevenage New Town, which has been ridden by increasing numbers of cyclists, those numbers swelled by some who have actually left their cars at home.

A final point, concerning money, which emerges from the Peak Park

Planning Board's 1977 investigatory survey of the Rowsley–Peak Forest line, is that it was estimated that it would cost them *more* to demolish or wall up the 27 bridges, 9 viaducts and 7 tunnels along the line (a total of £604,000) than it would do to fully repair them and subsequently maintain them for the first seven years in their care (£501,000). Durham County Council, which now has more viaducts open to pedestrians on its several railway walks than any other authority, has found the same principle in application. One can go on from this to say that, though the costs of land are now relatively far higher than in the early sixties, and despite the obvious fact that it costs much more to restore a route which has lain derelict for a decade than it would have done to take it over in its pristine railway state, conversions are still perfectly financially viable if they are handled in the right way. As councils have the first option they can purchase the line and then sell off station sites for light industrial or residential uses, keeping the track – *which is all that is needed*. This is well exemplified in the purchase by West Sussex County Council of twenty miles of line between Steyning and Rudgwick, where the cost of acquisition (£158,000) plus the cost of bridge works and surfacing (£39,000) was more than matched by freeholds, leaseholds and appropriations to other County Councils (£275,000 in all). For the first few years, that bridleway will not cost the local ratepayers even a fraction of a penny each. Now, if this could be done on a national basis. . . .

THE ACTUAL DEVELOPMENT OF ACCESS SCHEMES

A number of other writers and groups produced suggestions for the reuse of disused railways in the late sixties, amongst which may be noted the Railway Conversion League, which argued in vain for wholesale conversion into roads. Their paper 'No Alternative' (1965) states:

'. . . today the network is one of our most priceless possessions and, because the railways have been bought by the nation, it is a national heritage which must be retained at all costs and used to the fullest advantage.'

The most important and subsequently influential document produced was the Countryside Commission Report 'Disused Railways in the Countryside of England and Wales' (1970), prepared by Dr. J. H. Appleton, Reader in Geography at the University of Hull. The Countryside Commission was established in 1968 under the Countryside Act, taking over and extending the functions of the National Parks Commission, its activities polarising into matters of conservation of landscape beauty, and the provision of facilities for recreation in the countryside. The Appleton Report was produced in a matter of only six months, with the dual objectives of collecting data about disused railways and the various uses to which they were being or might be put, and helping the Countryside Commission to consider proposals by local authorities for the conversion of railways into recreational facilities. It is worth pointing out that if such a thoroughly researched piece of work could be drawn up in six months in 1969, it could equally well have been drawn up in 1963–4, under the initiation of the National Parks Commission, at a time when it would almost certainly have been far more directly useful. Why did it take six years for anybody to get around to requesting it? It should also be noted that the second objective of the Report is based upon the assumption that it should be, and will be, the responsibility of local planning authorities to propose conversion schemes, and not the responsibility of some centralised, Government-appointed body (the Countryside Commission itself?) which could effectively control the reuse of the 'formidable resource' of disused lines on a nationwide basis. Well, perhaps even in 1969 it was already too late for that. But it is hardly surprising that both the short and long term effects of Countryside Commission activity on disused lines has been nothing more than the funding of *fragmentary* conversions of generally isolated stretches of track from county to county as 'railway walks' and 'country parks'.

Indeed, one of the central recommendations that Appleton makes is that 'Councils set themselves up as the custodians of general public interest' (7.9), which had evidently not been the case previously except in isolated instances. He also suggests that it would be a good idea if local authorities were required 'to prepare plans for the subsequent use of all disused railways . . .' and make provision 'for *all* disused railways to be brought before the Countryside Commission at an early stage, so that guidance might be obtained on how the public interest may best be served' (7.13). He rejects as too drastic, I am sorry to say, the idea that a separate body should be set up 'to take over the process of disposal from the British Railways Board thereby relieving it of the obligation to seek the highest price in the market with the consequent disadvantages resulting from piecemeal sales' (7.12). But such 'drastic' measures were precisely what was required! The most Appleton has to say for the retention of the network is this: 'there is a certain logic in the view that, once land has been acquired in a form designed for use as some kind of communication, its linear integrity should be retained until it has been clearly established that no potential linear use can be justified in the public interest' (4.4). The majority of recreational redevelopments 'in the public interest' that followed were, of course, based precisely on such linear integrity.

It would be fair to say that the 1960s saw the coming to a head, at both a national and a local administrative level, of that revolution in awareness towards the use of the countryside for recreation which had been evolving in Britain since the end of the war: this is reflected in the various acts of Parliament passed – the Civic Amenities Act of 1967, the Town and Country Planning Act of 1968, and the Countryside Act. As a Ramblers Association paper, 'People and the Countryside', observed at the end of the decade, 'talk of the new wave of leisure and mobility is the commonplace of every environmental, planning and conservationist conference'. In the last two years of the decade the Countryside Commission received over 200 proposals from local authorities to create country parks (ten years later there are around 100 officially designated) – of which, of course, only a handful were based on disused railways. Most of us do not, I think, have quite such a large extra helping of leisure time as was being predicted then, but the facilities have nevertheless been made, and are continuing to be made.

The redevelopment of disused railways has, with certain exceptions, been along much the same lines as that of country parks, even where they have not been so designated and future developments seem likely to follow the same kind of pattern. As might be expected, old railways have been regarded by local authorities as just another resource of derelict land that can be used, like old gravel pits and woodlands, in sections, where convenient, either (where they do not resemble country parks) simply as an official confirmation of established use by locals as paths from one part of a town to another, or as facilities in the country near to towns, which can cater in several ways for a largely car-bound urban and suburban population who will drive to them, get out, sniff the air, and get back in again. Railways like the Wirral Country Park, the High Peak Trail, the Cole Green Way in Hertfordshire, the Derwent Walk in County Durham, the Forest and Worth Ways in Sussex, as well as redeveloped station sites like those at Tintern in Gwent or Clare in Suffolk, have been conceived as drive-in country entertainments, places to visit in the same way as one might visit any of the country parks made on sites such as commons, woodlands and the parks and gardens of stately homes. They are as experiences – despite the attempts in some places to link them with existing footpaths, and despite the fact that some do join one town with another – absolutely divorced from their original function as routes linking with other routes across the country, as bridleways connect with lanes, and lanes connect with other lanes. A very few stretches have been absorbed into long-distance Recreational Paths, for example the 7-mile Spa Trail in Lincolnshire is a part of the Viking Way, 2 miles of line has been incorporated into the Lower Wye Valley Walk in Gwent, another 1½ miles makes up part of the Staffordshire Way, but even then most of the rest of the lines in question remain unused as public routes. The segmentation involved in recreational development finds its most absurd example in the three separate paths between Sudbury and Lavenham.

The stated purposes of country parks are: 'to make it easier for dwellers in towns to spend their leisure in the open without travelling too far and adding to congestion on the roads; without crowding into places that depend for their appeal on remoteness and solitude; and without risking damage to agricultural interests' (information leaflet on the Countryside Commission). In other words they are breathing spaces, to which people can *drive*. I am not about to suggest that the country parks and related facilities have not answered a clearly defined need: this they have done. Instead of picnicking on the verges of main roads as so many used to do, people can now go to a country park, leave their car, get out and use their legs a little, at least, and picnic in clean air in a green place. Country parks have developed in direct response to the proliferation of the private car – and, one might also say, to the closure of the railways. They are, as a leaflet says, 'ideal if you only have a few hours to get out into the countryside' from a large town.

But there is more than one way of reading those stated aims. If the majority were to take the bait the country park offers, then who exactly would remain to benefit from the more difficult to reach 'places of remoteness and solitude'? It could be argued, I suppose, that people who are determined to walk in the depths of the country will do so anyway, country parks or no country parks, and further that the long-distance and recreational paths – for which we are very much the richer – have been created to satisfy their needs. I am not worried about such people: they can already take care of themselves. What worries me is the addiction of the majority of our population to motor travel, and the fact that if the temptation to do something easy exists – in the shape of a country park to which one can drive in order to go for a gentle stroll – then people will do the easy thing, even if they had been vaguely wondering whether they might not try something a little more energetic. Going for a long, revitalising walk takes organisation as well as determination: how much easier to slide one's incipient or emergent pot under the steering wheel and slope off to the country park. Apart from the newly-organised paths there are also 120,000 miles of public rights of way in England and Wales, a large proportion of which are field paths. Some people may get on to certain lengths of these from a country park start, but only on to certain lengths. The rest remain for that minority-which-should-not-be-a-minority to tread in where the farmers have ploughed them up, in anticipation of the time when they can close them altogether since – they can argue – they are not being sufficiently used! ('Rationalisation' of field paths is a stated aim of the National Farmers' Union.)

Country parks, then – and railways redeveloped for access either as or in imitation of country parks – act as substitutes for a more vigorous involvement with the country. The well-intended provision of facilities in them such as picnic areas with homogeneous wooden tables so that one does not have to sit on the nasty, dirty ground, toilets so that one does not have to pee in the open air in an undignified manner, notice boards and signposts telling one where to go, and leaflets telling one how long it will take and what to look at on the way, must create an experience similar in quality if not in detail to that of the urban municipal park, with some education for those who would like it. Only where commons have been taken over are country parks what the leaflet says they are: '*real* country virtually on your doorstep' (my italics): by being redeveloped in this way they become ersatz country, officially predigested natural environments for the elderly of all ages. (I do not, of course, dispute that they are a great boon for those who are genuinely helpless.) The very attempts to raise the awareness of visitors via leaflets on flora, fauna, or farming methods, must operate as a barrier to direct experience because like television they step between visitor and life, offering him yet more paternalistic interpretations of experience and cutting off at the root his desire to look for himself and make up his own mind. The presence of wardens where they are employed is very much a part of the same issue: the fact that there is a man in charge, however pleasant he may be as an individual, serves to remind the visitor that he is *not* in real country. What field path has a warden watching over it?

At the Cotswold Water Park I happened to notice a boy and girl getting out of the padded, carpeted interior of their Ford Cortina and walking along the converted stretch of railway there. The girl – she was perhaps eighteen – was wearing 'slacks' and not-quite high heels, the boy was wearing a velvet jacket and highly polished pavement shoes. Both walked (they might have been depressed for some reason, of course) in a lethargic, slumped kind of a way. Their forebear and mine, the ordinary worker on the land of a century and a half earlier, might have mistaken them for members of the aristocracy, strolling on the parterre after lunch. Instead of stimulating independence and the relegation of the motor car to the garage, country parks and related railway redevelopments are catering both for physical and mental podginess, and acting as incentives towards the continued mass use of the car.

Yet, it may be asked, how else does the present-day dweller in the metropolis or suburbia get out of it unless he goes by car, especially if he has a family? One answer is that there is still a rail network of sorts, which serves all the big cities and towns: and the current policy of allowing bicycles free on most services is very encouraging from this point of view. Another, as already argued, is the greenway, which (where disused railway lines do not exist) could perhaps be made out of especially selected motor roads, henceforth closed to traffic, bringing urban pathways into use where they already existed. Some old railways have in fact been converted for exactly this purpose, though none are in the biggest conurbations: so, for example, there is a path leading out of the eastern inner city area of Hull into open country, another old line leads out from the centre of Bishop Auckland in County Durham, the Stoke-on-Trent Greenway will eventually link the inner area of the town with hilly country to the north, and a current project in Leicester (put forward, be it noted once more, by local residents) is the opening of the Swannington line to public access – this runs close to the western side of the urban centre. As you will have gathered, the three lines investigated in Wolverhampton and Teesside, though making (or almost making) the vital link for sections of the populations, leave everything to be desired in terms of maintenance. But at least they exist: in other cities much could be done, and nothing is being done.

I return, once again, to what might have been. Instead of what we have – little bits and pieces of old lines being opened for use by local authorities, usually only after confronting difficulties which would not have been there when the lines first closed, such as the need to make compulsory purchase of sections sold before they knew they would be needed, the entrenched and fearful opposition of owners of adjoining land, the restoration of bridges that need never have been demolished, the reclamation of land that need never have returned to wilderness, the removal of rubbish that need never have been tipped – and their subsequent use by people who drive cars *to* them in order to get on to them . . . instead of this we might have had a health-, independence- and sanity-inducing network of through ways, centrally initiated and locally administrated thereafter. It was there for the taking. For all that there are many new plans for disused railways, the achievement by this piecemeal local action totals, at a generous estimate, only a few hundred miles of line now officially accessible. Compared with the 6000+ miles sold between 1948 and today, that really is not very much.

But what of 'what might be'? In the first place it is clear that wherever possible either by local council action or as a result of direct intervention by the Countryside Commission, work should be done to develop the remaining disused lines into *some* kind of network, both locally and nationally. Despite the criticism I have levelled at it over the non-use of the South Durham and Lancashire Union line, Durham County Council has proved itself out-standing amongst local authorities in its reclamation of the disused lines in its region. Apart from the four paths listed in the appendix which are already open, Durham has acquired five further stretches of line totalling almost 50 miles, most of which will be reclaimed as ways when the money is available. The ultimate aim is a 'countywide network of . . . countryside walks on former railway lines' (Planning Office information sheet). The Derwent Walk is one of these, and its eventual incorporation into a network will, I trust, deflect a certain number of people who would otherwise have simply driven to one of the car parks along it when it existed in isolation, into trying it as a real route, linking with other routes. A similar network is planned for Avon and North Somerset, specifically to provide cyclists with alternative routes to traffic-infested main roads and hilly back lanes. But what is being done in Durham, and may be done in Avon, should not be confined to those areas.

It is also clear that the development of greenways along disused railways out of urban areas should be given first priority wherever the land remains undeveloped, and that cycle access should be mandatory. A Countryside Commission working paper, 'Cycling To The Countryside' (WP10, 1978), has made a specific recommendation (4.28) that disused railways be reclaimed as part of a civilised and civilising new policy – by no means yet implemented – to improve access to the country for cyclists living in urban areas. In all of the four study areas, Crewe, Bedford, Gloucester and Hull, suggestions are made for such reuse. In Hull – and also in Gloucester – no fewer than five stretches of line are isolated (5.24: three of these are already being used, as noted earlier and in the Appendix), and it is also wisely suggested that the length to Skirlaugh on the Hornsea branch could be redeveloped back into the centre of the town (5.23), which is in fact what has happened.

I would further suggest that the existing expensive pattern of redevelop-ment of bits of line here and there as drive-in entertainments be halted wherever there is a chance that the lines could in the future be used as through routes. Similarly, if long-distance greenways were to be created, they should be created *without* car parks, since car parks encourage an inappropriate kind of use, and also without toilets, homogeneous picnic tables, signs, leaflets, slide-shows, guided tours, or any of that paraphernalia of the country parks by which the country is being cosily suburbanised. Let us confine all that to the reclaimed gravel-pits, and try to get back to the spirit of independence which so very many urban men possessed before their children were robbed of it by the car.

I will reiterate here then, that there are a number of lines amongst those I explored for this book which would still make excellent greenways, though there would be problems in the conversion of each and every one of them. In particular the Bridport Railway, the Didcot, Newbury and Southampton, the Cleobury Mortimer and Ditton Priors, the South Durham and Lancashire Union, the Bala and Festiniog and the Brecon and Merthyr from the Cefn Coed viaduct to the Pontsticill reservoir, would make outstanding routes. No plans exist in any of the relevant planning departments for such redevelopment.

And what of future railway closures? What of the Hastings to Ashford line in Kent, or the Exeter to Barnstaple line in Devon, or the Milford Haven to Haverfordwest line in Pembrokeshire? These routes, as any of their users reading this book well know, are still operational and long may they remain so. They are, however, among the 41 lines totalling some 900 miles of track singled out for closure by the British Railways Board's Corporate Review of August 1979. The closure proposals, leaked by the *Guardian* on November 7th 1979, were subsequently vetoed by the Transport Minister Mr. Norman Fowler in a letter to the British Rail chairman in which he stated that it was his firm policy that there should be no substantial cuts in the passenger network. Even so, firm policy or no firm policy, British Rail is currently faced with a cut of £22 millions in Government subsidies to its passenger services; and the closure of the 41 provincial lines was the only remedy for this situation proposed in the corporate review, other than massive increases in already massively high fares. The danger for these lines remains, then, and the spectre of possible closure must hang over them even if some short-term financial remedy is found, at least until such time as the, theoretically, more economic railbus has been successfully developed – and indeed until the day that the current Government's public spending policy has been diametrically and unequivocally reversed. The spectre hangs over the remaining 44 of the other Provincial Services, totalling a further 1100 miles of track, which are also threatened, in the nicest possible way, by the conclusion of the August 1979 review where it is stated that in the long term yet further service withdrawals would help to reduce the size of government subsidy to passenger services. (Extend this crazy logic one more step, of course, and you are left with the perfect solution to the embarrassing problem of subsidy: the closure of the rail network in its entirety.)

There are then in all some 2000 miles of railway line in England, Wales and Scotland which might eventually, by the application of insanely destructive public spending cuts by this or future Governments, and by desperate negative thinking by the British Railways Board, be transformed from discrete interlinked transport routes into heath, wild wood, rubbish tip and bonfire site. None of us who have the slightest regard for either the environment or the railways wants this to happen. But let us imagine that it did happen. Is there, even now, any mechanism by which such land could be saved for the nation of individuals who (so long as it remains in the hands of British Rail) nominally own it? There is not, and there should be; and it must be the responsibility of the Countryside Commission to create such a mechanism without further delay. It does not matter if in the short term this takes the form of nothing more than a safety net whereby the British Rail Property Board is required to keep derelict land created by future closures within its possession. What does matter is that the routes should be *preserved intact* until such time as they can be transformed into greenways by a centralised body – a department of the Countryside Commission created for this purpose – for the benefit of the public as a whole.

I have one final suggestion relating to the reuse of old railways for – in a sense – recreational purposes, and this is that in many places near towns or villages they could be used for allotments. With waiting periods for allotments in some areas of several years, this would seem to be not only a rational reuse of derelict land but a highly productive one. The single example I have seen of allotments on old railway land is at Norton in North Yorkshire, but upon enquiring I found – as I rather expected – that this had not been the brainchild of the local council, and that allotment holders had previously been tenants of British Rail (though the land cultivated appears to have been extended since the line closed). Elsewhere, on the Swindon–Cricklade line, someone had started a long, narrow and very successful garden along the side of an embankment, but I doubt very much whether this either had anything to do with bureaucratic initiative. The enormity of the leeks on this strip could act as effective testimony against any prevaricatory arguments that 'railway land is unproductive'. Why should old lines *just* be used as gardeners' compost-heaps?

WILL THE RAILWAYS EVER BE REOPENED?

'As soon as the required procedure permits, it is desired to withdraw those passenger train services which are clearly uneconomic. . . . In most cases there will eventually be no passenger service of any description over the lines affected.'

('The Reshaping of British Railways' – the 'Beeching Report', p. 97.)

   '. . . *I am in blood*

> *Stepp'd in so far that, should I wade no more,*
> *Returning were as tedious as go o'er.'*
> *(Shakespeare, 'Macbeth' III, iv, 136.)*

You may reflect on the fall of empires as you roam disused railway lines, but you may also dream of their resurrection. Amongst the several organisations to have advocated at various times that the linear integrity of closed lines be retained is the Council for the Protection of Rural England. Their view is that there may well be a case for reopening at such time as we finally run out of oil, if some more economic form of mass transport using the old routes can be devised. The National Council on Inland Transport has made similar suggestions. The Ecologist's 'Blueprint for Survival' argues that 'broadly speaking the only alternative', to the massive increase in road use 'is public transport – a mix of rapid mass-transit by road and rail', noting also that 'the power requirements for transporting freight by road are five to six times greater than by rail and the pollution is correspondingly higher' (p, 55).

Two fundamental assumptions underlay the advocacy of the closure of railways in the Beeching Report. The first is that they should pay their own way, and not depend upon government subsidy: the second, even more questionable now, is that 'it is no longer socially necessary for the railways to cover such a preponderant part of the total variety of internal transport as they did in the past' (Foreword, p. 4). But in what sense 'no longer socially necessary'? Was there not and is there not a clear social need to keep freight away from the roads in order to preserve both lives and living environments? And how is that possible except via the closed-circuit routing that railways provide? Also, even if the need in 1963 to encourage people to use public transport instead of the private car was not absolutely clear (and surely it was becoming clearer and clearer) it certainly is now: regular, cheap (subsidised) bus services may provide a part of the answer, but only a part. The one other means of tempting people off the roads is the railway passenger service – the regular, cheap, *increasingly* subsidised railway passenger service. It would be interesting though in practise probably impossible to compare the savings made for the railways by the Beeching cuts with the corresponding increase in expenditure on road building and maintenance, especially in country areas, to take the traffic thus re-routed. My guess is that the latter would far outweigh the former.

Recommendations on possible nationwide transport reuse may have been made, but who paid, or pays, any attention? Certainly not British Rail, and local authorities only in very isolated instances. The Isle of Wight County Council, as a rare example, keeps control of all the disused lines on the island –

and is in the process of converting them into footpaths in the meantime – 'in order to be in a position to take advantage of any technological breakthrough in mass transportation' (County Structure Plan).

There are, again, isolated instances of lines having been closed, or nearly closed, and then reopened. The 'Dales Rail' scheme, for example, was initiated in 1974 by the Yorkshire Dales National Park Committee to bring back a passenger service to closed stations between Settle and Carlisle on the former Midland line to Scotland (which was in fact never completely closed, remaining open for express services after the stopping trains were withdrawn in 1969). Under this scheme derelict stations (including one at Kirkby Stephen) were restored by the Park Committee, and an experimental charter rail service was brought into operation to serve both those who wanted to get away from the hills to do their shopping and those who wanted to get on to them to walk. A local bus service provided links with nearby towns. The scheme operated successfully in 1975–8, but is now jeopardised by the increasingly high charter charges imposed by British Rail and the National Bus Company. Another resuscitation, by industry, is that of a section of the old Saltburn–Whitby line in North Yorkshire, which was completely closed in 1958, then reopened in 1969 by Cleveland Potash to serve a mine at Old Boulby. This involved the construction of a new rail-over-road viaduct, and the filling of an embankment which had been excavated following the original closure.

Even when there is death there may at times be hope. But if no examples existed of reopening, it would still be true to say that the *possibility* of reopening lines in future should have been considered at length, at government level – and not just by the County Council of the Isle of Wight. If this possibility had been considered in the light, or darkness, of the subsequent growth of road transport and all related problems, we would surely still have that network intact.

One final reflection, at a time when the oil companies are moving into Surrey and Dorset in desperate search of the last few dribbles of oil the earth can give us (will there be an oil rig in Hardy's cottage garden at Bockhampton?) – is that in a century's time, God willing, we may be exploring disused motorways, or that instead of forty-tonners and plastic service areas there may be asses and mules, and half-timbered caravanserai, along some routes long since converted back to beaten earth. These islands are already a repository of disused routes – the sheep-drove mountain tracks, the Roman roads, the bridle roads, as well as the disused railways. It has yet to be seen whether all the old ·railways will remain forever in that good company. And especially must we be hopeful now that British Rail has finally found a way of working transport miracles: I have a current edition of the Thames Traveller Timetable which shows quite clearly and with absolute certainty that, if you catch the right connection, you can arrive at Slough before you have left Paddington.

Once a railway: the Ditton Priors branch.

Once a railway: the A40 west of Monmouth.

Once a prehistoric 'trunk' route: the Ridgeway Path, on Blewbury Down.

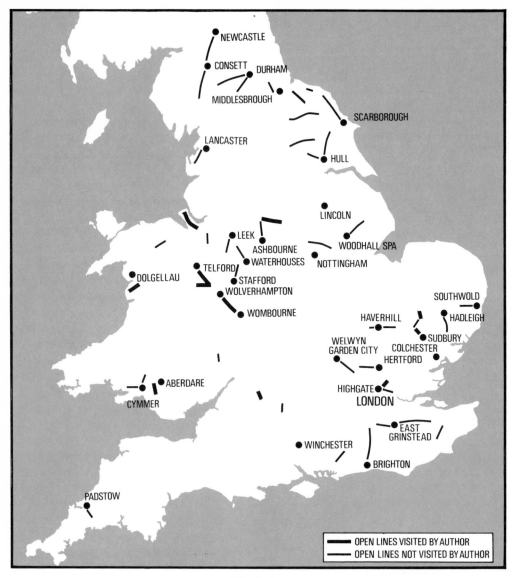

DISUSED RAILWAYS OPEN TO THE PUBLIC AS PATHS

This map shows the approximate location of the stretches of line mentioned in the appendix. The list is in the first place selective, and may be guilty of other omissions: nevertheless the map gives a workable impression of what has so far been achieved.

APPENDIX: A SELECT LIST OF DISUSED RAILWAYS IN ENGLAND AND WALES NOW OFFICIALLY OPEN TO THE PUBLIC AS PATHS:

Only stretches already open, or at present very close to being opened, are included in this list. Neither picnic areas (etc.) on isolated sites nor the majority of very short lengths are mentioned. All tracks also covered in the book are emphasised with grey blocks. Note that in these cases there is some divergence between the lengths of line open and the lengths I actually explored. Where access is stated as being only available to walkers this does not necessarily mean that cyclists and horse riders are formally kept out, or that revisions will not later be made by the councils concerned.

LOCATION c = Cyclists	NAME OF WALK (*Where named*) h = Horse-riders	LENGTH (*in miles*) w = Walkers	ACCESS	ORDNANCE (*I: 50,000*) *Map no.*
ENGLAND				
CHESHIRE				
1. Winsford Junction– Catsclough	Whitegate Way	6	w,h	118
CLEVELAND				
2. Hartburn-Hardwick		3	w	93
3. South Bank– Normanby		1½	w	93
CORNWALL				
4. Padstow– Wadebridge		5½	w, trial access for c and h	200
DERBYSHIRE				
5. Cromford-Dowlow	High Peak Trail	17½	w,c,h	119
6. Ashbourne–Parsley Hay	Tissington Trail	13	w,c,h	119
7. Hayfield–New Mills	Sett Valley Trail	3	w,c,h	110
COUNTY DURHAM				
8. Swalwell-Consett	Derwent Walk	10½	w,c,h	88
9. Consett-Waskerley	Waskerley Way	7	w,c,h	87/88
10. Crook-Durham	Deerness Valley Walk	9	w,c,h	92/88
11. Durham-Bishop Auckland	Bishop-Brandon Walk	9½	w,c,h	92/93
ESSEX				
12. Wivenhoe-Bright- lingsea		3	w	168
GLOUCESTERSHIRE				
13. at South Cerney	Cotswold Water Park	1½	w,c	163

LOCATION	NAME OF WALK (*Where named*)	LENGTH (*in miles*)	ACCESS	ORDNANCE (*1: 50,000*) Map no.
HAMPSHIRE				
14. Litchfield-Highclere		3	w,c,h	185 & 174
15. Knowle Junct.- West Meon		9	w,c,h	196 & 185
HERTFORDSHIRE				
16. Hertford-Cole Green	Cole Green Way	4	w,c,h	166
17. Wheathampstead- Welwyn Garden City	Ayot Greenway	4	w,c,h	166
HUMBERSIDE				
18. Market Weighton- Cherry Burton	Market weighton Way	9	w,c,h	106
19. Hull-Skirlaugh		13	w,c	107
20. Hull-Cottingham		1	w,c	107
LANCASHIRE				
21. Glasson Dock- Aldcliffe	Lune Estuary Footpath	3½	w	102
LINCOLNSHIRE				
22. Woodhall Spa- Horncastle	Spa Trail, section of the Viking Way	7	w,c,h	122
LONDON				
23. Highgate-Alexandra Palace	Parkland Walk	1	w,c	176
24. Highgate Finsbury Park		2	w,c	176
MERSEYSIDE (and CHESHIRE)				
25. West Kirby-Hooton	Wirral Country Park	12	w,h	108 & 117
NOTTINGHAMSHIRE				
26. Farnsfield-Southwell	Southwell Trail	5½	w,c,h	120
SHROPSHIRE				
27. Coalport-Telford	Silkin Way	4	w,c	127
28. Coalport-Ironbridge	South Bank Footpath	3	w	127
STAFFORDSHIRE				
29. Castlecroft-Himley	Kingswinford Branch Railway Walk	5½	w,c,h	139
30. Leek-Rushton Spencer	(Staffordshire Way runs along 1½ m.)	5½	w,h	118
31. Stoke-on-Trent to Goldenhill	Potteris Greenway	6	w,c	118
32. Waterhouses-Hulme End		8½	w,h	119
SUFFOLK				
33. Hadleigh-Raydon		2½	w	155
34. at Haverhill	Railway Walk	2	w	154

LOCATION	NAME OF WALK (*Where named*)	LENGTH (*in miles*)	ACCESS	ORDNANCE (*1: 50,000*) *Map no.*
35. at Lavenham	Lavenham Walk	1½	w	155
36. at Long Melford	Melford Walk	1	w	155
37. Sudbury-Rodbridge Corner	Valley Walk	2	w	155
38. Southwold-Blythburgh		3½	w,h	156
SUSSEX (EAST)				
39. East Grinstead-Groombridge	Forest Way	9	w,c,h	187 & 188
40. Heathfield-Polegate	Cuckoo Walk	10	w	199
SUSSEX (WEST)				
41. East Grinstead-Worth	Worth Way (continuous with above)	6	w,c,h	187
42. Steyning-Rudgwick	(links with South Downs Way)	18	w,h,	198 & 187
WEST MIDLANDS				
43. Aldersley-Castlecroft	Valley Park	3	w	139
YORKSHIRE (NORTH)				
44. at Sandsend	section of Cleveland Way	1	w	94
45. Ingleby Greenhow-Farndale Moor	section of Lyke Wake Walk	6½	w	94
46. Scarborough-Hawkser		13	w,c,h	101
WALES				
CLWYD				
47. at Glyn Ceiriog	Glyn Valley Tramway	1	w	125
GLAMORGAN (MID)				
48. Cwmaman-Dare Valley		3	w	170
GLAMORGAN (WEST)				
49. Glyncorrwg-Cymmer	Afan Valley Greenway	3	w	170
50. Cymmer-Blaengwynfi	Afan Valley Greenway	3	w	170
GWENT				
51. Redbrook-Whitebrook	section of Wye Valley Walk	2	w	162
52. Govilon-Llanfoist		3	w	161
GWYNEDD				
53. Penmaenpool-Arthog		4	w	124

FURTHER READING GENERAL HISTORIES

The 'Regional History of the Railways' (vols I–IX) published by David & Charles, and their 'Forgotten Railways' series (seven books) give detailed information on many of the lines mentioned in this book.

There are also a number of histories of the bigger railway companies, which tend to be monumental works, and not the kind of book that is easily portable in a rucksack or pocket. I found the following particularly useful:

E. T. Macdermot, 'History of the Great Western Railway,' vols. I–II, pub. Ian Allan, revised ed. 1964

W. W. Tomlinson, 'The North Eastern Railway: its Rise and Development', republished as 'Tomlinson's North Eastern Railway', David & Charles, 1967

SINGLE LINES

'The Bridport Branch', M. J. Tattershall and B. L. Jackson, Oxford Publishing, 1976

'The Somerset and Dorset Railway', Robin Atthill, David & Charles, 1970

'The Midland and South West Junction Railway,' T. B. Sands, Oakwood Press, 1959

'The Didcot, Newbury and Southampton Railway,' T. B. Sands, Oakwood Press, 1971

'By Rail to Wombourn', J. Ned Williams, Uralia Press, 1967

'The Cleobury Mortimer and Ditton Priors Railway', W. H. Smith and K. Beddoes, Oxford Press, 1980

'The Severn Valley Railway', D. J. Smith, Town and Country Press, 1970

'The Cromford and High Peak Railway', A. Rimmer, Oakwood Press, 1967

'The Brecon and Merthyr Railway,' D. S. M. Barrie, Oakwood Press, 1957

MAPS AND RELATED INFORMATION

'British Railways Pre-Grouping Atlas and Gazetteer', W. Philip Conolly, pub. Ian Allan, reprinted 1972, shows the lines of every British railway company operating up to 1923.

'Sectional Maps of British Railways', (no author credited), Ian Allan, 1967, is a companion to the above, in which its maps are reprinted to show the situation in 1967. Closed lines are marked in yellow. Though out of date, this is the best volume available for instant identification of disused lines.

'Rail Atlas of Britain', S. K. Baker, Oxford Publishing Co., 1978, gives an almost up-to-date picture of all lines still in use, whether for passenger, goods, industrial or preservationist purposes.

'Passengers No More,' G. Daniels and L. A. Dench, Ian Allan, 1965, lists all lines closed to that date, with dates of closure. Recently revised.

'The Reshaping of British Railways', HMSO, 1963. Part II contains a series of maps relating to closure and modification of services.

THE PROBLEM OF REUSE

Most important amongst the material that I have mentioned or drawn upon is:

J. H. Appleton, for the Countryside Commission, 'Disused Railways in the Countryside of England and Wales', H.M.S.O., 1970

Countryside Commission, 'Schemes for Recreational Use of Disused Railways', 1971

The Cyclists' Touring Club, 'The Cyclists' Case – An Early Plea', C.T.C. 1969/73

J. W. Davidson, 'An Examination of Disused Railways and their Future' (thesis), University College, London, 1975

M. Dower, 'Green Ways – A Positive Future for Britain's Cast-Off Railways?' article in 'Architectural Review', December 1963, p. 387

R Jarman, 'The Railways of Dorset – Their Relevance to Wildlife Conservation' (thesis), University College, London, 1974

C. E. M. Joad, 'The Untutored Townsman's Invasion of the Country', Faber, 1946

The Ramblers' Association, 'People and the Countryside', R.A., 1970

INTERESTED ORGANISATIONS

You may want to make enquiries, or suggestions, about the subject of access to disused railways. The first body to approach in any particular case would be the local council, but the following organisations have stated interests:

The British Horse Society, National Equestrian Centre, Stoneleigh, Kenilworth, Warwickshire. CV8 2LR

Commons, Open Spaces and Footpaths Preservation Society, 166 Shaftsbury Avenue, London WC2H 8JH

The Council for the Protection of Rural England, 4 Hobart Place, London SW1W 0HY

The Countryside Commission, John Dower House, Crescent Place, Cheltenham, Gloucestershire. GL50 3RA

The Cyclists' Touring Club, Cotterell House, 69 Meadrow, Godalming, Surrey. GU7 3HS

The Nature Conservancy, 19 Belgrave Square, London SW1

The Railway Ramblers (A club formed for the exploration of disused railways), 11 Milverton Avenue, Leicester.

The Ramblers' Association, 1/4 Crawford Mews, York Street, London W1H 1PT

The Youth Hostels Association, Trevelyan House, St. Albans, Hertfordshire, AL1 2DY

ACKNOWLEDGEMENTS

My thanks firstly to all the people mentioned in the book who spent time telling me about their own local disused railway.

My thanks for answering written queries and supplying documentation to officers of the following planning departments:

COUNTY COUNCILS. Bedfordshire, Berkshire, Cheshire, Cleveland, Cornwall, Cumbria, Devon, Durham, East Sussex, Essex, Gloucestershire, Gwent, Gwynedd, Hampshire, Hertfordshire, Humberside, Isle of Wight, Lancashire, Lincolnshire, Mid Glamorgan, North Yorkshire, Nottinghamshire, Salop, Staffordshire, Suffolk, West Glamorgan, West Sussex.

DISTRICT OR BOROUGH COUNCILS. Boothferry, Bridgnorth, Cynon Valley, Harborough, Haringey, Meirionnydd, Merthyr Tydfil, Newbury, North Norfolk, Ryedale, Scarborough, Sedgemoor, South Staffordshire, Thamesdown, Vale of White Horse, West Dorset, Wolverhampton.

NATIONAL PARKS. Brecon Beacons, Peak, Snowdonia, North York Moors, and the Peak National Park Youth and Schools Service.

COPYRIGHT

Faber and Faber for the quotations from C. E. M. Joad's 'The Untutored Townsman's Invasion of the Country'

The Cyclists' Touring Club for the quotation from 'Disused Railway Lines – the Cyclists' Case'

The Ramblers' Association for the quotation from 'People and the Countryside'

The Wirral Country Park for quotations from the information document on the Park

The County Council of the Isle of Wight for the quotation from the County Structure Plan

The Ecologist for the quotation from the 'Blueprint for Survival'

Oxford Publishing Co. for the quotation from B. L. Jackson's and M. J. Tattershall's 'The Bridport Branch'

I am indebted also to the following organisations and individuals for supplying me with information: Brecon Mountain Railway Co. (Mr. A. J. Hills), British Rail Property Board Public Relations Department (Mr. T. Warburton), British Railways Eastern Region (Mr. A. J. Ives), Campaign Against the Criminal Trespass Law (Mr. David Watkinson), Council for the Protection of Rural England (Mr. A. F. Holford-Walker), Cyclists' Touring Club (Mr. Leslie C. Warner), National Farmers' Union (Mr. R. B. Ellison), National Trust (Mr. I. F. Blomfield), Nature Conservancy Council Library Service (Mr. M. N. Tither), Northumbrian Water Authority (Mr. Tom Buffey and Mr. John Richards), Railway Ramblers (Mr. Nigel Willis), Ramblers Association (Mr. John Newnham), Stour Valley Railway Preservation Society (Mr. M. C. Stanbury), Sudbury-Marks Tey Rail Users' Association (Mr. Mike Davies), Swindon and Cricklade Railway Society (Mr. Reg Palk), Telford Development Corporation (Mr. F. Clamp), Wessex Water Authority (Mr. B. A. Tinkler), Wirral County Park (Mr. E. D. Jarvis and Mr. Frank White), Youth Hostels Association (Mr. Roger Clarke).

In particular I would like to thank Mr. Paul Davison, Transport Engineer of the Countryside Commission, for his many patient replies to an unending stream of questions; Mr. T. J. Edgington, Technical Information Officer of the National Railway Museum for supplying a most useful and relevant bibliography as well as technical information; Mr. Reg Stanley and Mr. Gerald McDonald of the Telford (Horsehay) Steam Trust for much guidance, filling of gaps and correcting of technical mistakes; Mr. M. J. Tattershall for supplying information on the Bridport Branch; and to Mr. K. Beddoes for supplying information on the Cleobury Mortimer and Ditton Priors Light Railway.